Inside the Ancient World

D0580827

THE GREEK AND ROMAN STAGE

INSIDE THE ANCIENT WORLD
General Editor: Michael Gunningham

The following titles are available in this series:

*Denotes books which are especially suited to GCSE or studies at a comparable 16+ level. The remainder may be useful at that level, but can also be used by students on more advanced courses.

Inside the Ancient World

THE GREEK AND ROMAN STAGE

David Taylor

BRISTOL CLASSICAL PRESS
General Editor: Michael Gunningham

Published in 1999 by
Bristol Classical Press
an imprint of
Gerald Duckworth & Co. Ltd
61 Frith Street
London W1V 5TA

A catalogue record for this book is available
from the British Library

ISBN 1-85399-591-6

Printed in Great Britain by
Antony Rowe Ltd

WITHDRAWN

Contents

Preface

This volume was first published in the series *Greek and Roman Topics* under the title *Acting and the Stage*. I have taken the opportunity of this revised edition to change and update the material.

As in the original volume, limitations of space impose compression, and on occasion conclusions are more tentative than the text may suggest. However, where a major point relies on guesswork or invention, this is stated.

I should like to record grateful thanks to Mrs. Pat Easterling of Newnham College, Cambridge, for many helpful suggestions (though she cannot be held responsible for any of the views expressed); to my wife, Pamela, whose practical experience of the theatre and assistance in the preparation and revision of the manuscript have been invaluable; and to Dr. Barbara Goward and Prof. Oliver Taplin for advice on recent developments in scholarship.

Acknowledgements

Permission to reproduce illustrations, as in the original version, is gratefully acknowledged as follows:
British Museum: 16, 21, 29, 30; the Mansell Collection: 3, 4, 5, 6, 7, 11, 12, 13, 15, 18, 19, 22, 24, 25, 26, 27, 28, 31, 32, 33, 34; David Raeburn, 17; Warburg Institute, University of London: 9, 10.

Illustrations

1
How the Greek theatre began

What is the theatre?

The word 'theatre', found in many European languages, is from the Greek for 'see' or 'watch'. 'Drama' also comes from a Greek word, meaning 'do'. In its most basic sense, then, the theatrical experience is about *watching something which is done*. So we have *spectators* (this time from the Latin root) who watch, and *actors* who 'do' (again, Latin) or perform.

If the drama is an 'action', it is also, essentially, one performed in *words*, but also through movement, gesture, expression, and often music. (A play without words is a 'pantomime', not a drama in this sense.) Drama, therefore, is in important ways a form of literature and shares many features with, for example, an epic poem or a novel. Some playwrights even wrote without any serious intention of seeing their plays performed, such as the Roman Seneca (see Chapter 5) and even to some extent the Norwegian Henrik Ibsen, who often referred to his plays as 'texts' and the audience as 'readers'. A play need not, of course, ever be performed and readers of the text can certainly appreciate it from the printed page – as practised musicians can 'hear' the written score of a symphony which has never been played. But most of us need to hear the dialogue of human voices and their expression, just as, at least for most of us, the musical notes of a symphony need to be interpreted in performance if we are to gain the full effect and interplay of the instruments. Both plays and musical works are completely realised only when they are performed.

The stage

The 'stage' is the name we give to the area where the actors perform. It is the word used in the title of this book to remind us of the fact that the theatre is essentially a performance by actors, and not simply a written text. The stage separates the actors from the spectators and it therefore represents a different 'world'. What actors perform on this stage is, we know, in some ways not a *real* event, but it has its own reality and it invites those who watch to participate in this world. In Shakespeare's play *Henry V*, for example, the 'Chorus' (a term taken from the ancient Greek theatre, incidentally) apologises to the spectators for the inadequacies of his stage – the 'wooden O' – and invites them to use their imaginations:

On your imaginary forces work,
Suppose within the girdle of these walls
Are now confin'd two mighty monarchies….

It is worth noting that English refers to a theatrical performance as a 'play', just as Latin did ('ludus'), and we use 'play-acting' as a way of saying that someone is not expressing what is real but is creating a pretence, or a representation. The Greek word for the actor has also passed into modern European languages: it gives the English word 'hypocrite', by which we mean someone who is insincere, who 'strikes a pose' or 'wears a mask'.

In order to understand what going to the theatre is, it is vital to be able to separate the *actor*, who is a real person with his or her own traits, appearance and voice, from the *character* (a Greek word) or *persona* (Latin) portrayed on stage. We expect the actor to be portraying someone else, and also that the action we watch is not, in the end, 'real'. When characters on stage fight, we do not look for real blood: what we expect is to feel convinced that it is a fight fought for 'real' human motives and with persuasive emotions; the actors make us believe in the events we witness while at the same time knowing they are not actual events. This ability to believe and yet not believe what we are seeing is a fundamental part of the theatre-going experience.

Throughout the history of the theatre, this line has at times been blurred deliberately: the ancient Romans showed real deaths on stage – at the final curtain, these corpses did not stand up and take a bow; there was no acting here. The Greek theatre, however, did not permit much of the 'action' to which we are accustomed on stage – murders or violent acts, especially, were almost invariably committed off-stage. It is from this fact that we have the word, again common in modern European languages, 'obscene' – that which should not be shown on stage (Greek: *skene*).

The beginnings of the theatre

Many books have been written about how the theatre began and the explanations which they give are not always the same, since the origins are buried in the early history of human civilisation. It is impossible to tell exactly where the idea of performing in front of other people first came from. What is clear is that for the Western world it was the ancient Greeks who were responsible for the origins and development of the theatre. (There are also strong and ancient theatrical traditions in other countries, including the Japanese Noh and Kabuki traditions.) Even though there are areas of uncertainty about these beginnings, there is a variety of evidence, including that which comes from the surviving plays themselves.

Examining the evidence

The Greek playwrights do not always give us as much evidence for the origins of the theatre as we might hope: they were, of course, writing plays, not a history. Other Greek writers, such as historians (for the Greeks invented history, as well as the theatre), are sometimes useful, but not as often as we would like. Greek historians dealt mainly with wars and politics.

Much of the most useful information comes, in fact, from Greek art and architecture. A large number of theatre buildings survive, often in a remarkably good state of repair, from all around the areas in which the Greeks settled – especially modern Turkey. There are many examples of painted vases and sculpture which date from around the time when the theatre began, and occasionally these refer to theatrical productions; a number of illustrations in this book are taken from these sources.

Greek art

Figure 1 shows a vase from the area around Athens, the city where all the great Greek playwrights lived. Several vases were made around 500 BC (i.e. in the very early days of the theatre) which show groups of men dressed up in bird or animal costumes to take part in revels – dancing and general merry-making. Here, a man plays a small wind instrument (like a double oboe), accompanying two dancers dressed in a costume with wings, feathers and a bird's head. Choruses of costumed dancers therefore go back to the beginnings of the theatre, and clearly they contributed to its development. Nearly a hundred years later than this vase-painting, a play called *The Birds* (a Greek comedy by Aristophanes) had a chorus wearing outfits very similar to these. The play survives today, and costumes from a twentieth century production of it formed a prominent part of a recent exhibition called 'A Stage for Dionysus', at the Theatre Museum in London.

Inscriptions

We can also look at Greek inscriptions. These are records inscribed on stone, some of which contain important historical information about plays and playwrights and the years when plays were first produced. Sometimes complete inscriptions still exist; there are also many fragments, such as that in Figure 2.

This fragment is part of a list, called *The Athenian Victors' List*, which records the names of winners in the dramatic competitions at Athens. There are no complete names on this portion, but scholars have been able to work out some interesting facts. The Greek capital letters are very clear. The top line has the letters ΣXY, the middle letters of the name Ae**schy**lus. (The Greek alphabet is given in Appendix II.) The fifth line reads ΚΛΗΣ ΔΠΙΙΙ. This is the end of the name Sophocles, and after the name are Greek numerals – ten, five and three ones, totalling eighteen.

1. *Chorus of men in bird-costumes, dancing to the music of a flute player; after an Athenian black-figured* oenochoe *(wine-jug) of about 480 BC by the Gela Painter. [British Museum, London (no. B509)]*

Aeschylus and Sophocles are two of the most famous Greek playwrights, and these records clearly refer to them. The Victors' List went back about ten years before the name Aeschylus, though the first few entries cannot be read now. A later Greek writer says that Aeschylus won his first victory in the playwrights' competition of about 484 BC, and this fits other information in the records. We also know that Sophocles won his first victory later than Aeschylus, and the evidence from the Victors' List shows that altogether he won eighteen victories.

Figures 1 and 2 represent just two examples of evidence from Greek art and inscriptions. There are many others, which can be placed alongside the writings of the Greeks and the surviving remains of the theatre buildings. While it is possible in this way to build up a reasonably full picture of the early days of the theatre, there are still some things about which we cannot be sure, because the evidence is inconclusive.

Greek festivals

A festival is a regular celebration of an important event, normally a religious event. Our best-known annual festivals are such religious celebrations as

Christmas, Hanukkah or Diwali. They are times when no work is done, and often include great processions through the streets, with dancing, drinking and general merriment, although they can also have more solemn elements. Sometimes a statue of the saint or god to whom the festival is dedicated is carried through the streets. In Greece and Italy, as in other Mediterranean countries, there are still many annual festivals, just as there were in the times

2. *The Athenian Victors' List*

of the ancient Greeks and Romans. For the Greeks, these religious festivals were also great social, political and civic events for the citizens, for whom it offered an opportunity to celebrate the achievements of the people publicly.

In Greece, as in Japan and in other traditions, the origins of theatrical performance are intimately linked to religion. The Greek theatre was a central element in the festivals of Dionysus, god of wine and fertility: annually there were four of these in Athens, the *Anthesteria,* the *Lenaia*, the *Country Dionysia* and the *Great Dionysia*, as well as large numbers of smaller local festivals. Greek drama grew up from these celebrations. It is thought that the city of Athens held more state festivals of this kind than any other place in Ancient Greece. Some commentators refer to Athens as having a 'performance culture', in which political life had theatrical elements, and theatrical festivals certainly had a political as well as religious character. The Assembly, where democratic meetings took place, began with animal sacrifices as did the theatrical festival presentations. The citizens of Athens participated fully in all these events, sharing in the sacred rituals.

Dionysus

There were many stories about the god Dionysus, and these myths formed part of the background to the Greek plays; one of the most famous of these is in *The Bacchants* by Euripides. Dionysus, according to myth, was the son of

Zeus but not by his wife, the goddess Hera. Zeus had many affairs with mortal women and one of these was Semele, the mother of Dionysus. In anger, Hera had Semele killed by the thunderbolt of Zeus; but Zeus rescued Semele's unborn child, and hid him from Hera in his thigh, from where he was eventually born. Dionysus became one of the most frequently worshipped of all the Greek gods – as the number of cults and festivals dedicated to him show.

3. *Exekias Cup: Dionysus on a boat. [Staatliche Antikensammlungen, Munich]*

Dionysus is often shown in paintings as the god of wine, like the Roman god Bacchus. He is either drinking wine or surrounded by grapes. This was one of his main characteristics for the ancient Greeks, but he was much more also. He was especially connected with fertility, whether human birth or the fruitfulness of the land, and with nature in its wild forms. Many early religious festivals are associated with sowing seed or gathering in the crops; and such events were particularly important to the ancient Greeks, who lived almost completely on agricultural produce, in a land which is not very fertile. Everything depended on a good harvest in the small cultivated plains which lay between the barren mountains.

The most important of the festivals was the Great Dionysia. This was held every year around the end of March, when the seas were open to sailing again after the winter storms. It was a grand occasion in Athens and people came from all over Greece to take part. This festival was the main time when a full programme of plays was presented, although both the Country Dionysia and the Lenaia also included some.

Dionysus had crowds of devoted followers, who were known as the *thiasos*. These followers traditionally included the band of women called *Bacchants* or *Maenads*. At certain times of year, it was said, these women abandoned their homes, ran to the mountains and took part in frenzied worship of their god. The climax was, so the traditional myths had it, a meal of raw flesh. The followers of Dionysus believed that by eating this they lost their own personalities and took on the power and person of the god. The worshippers often wore masks, and the image of the god was in the form of a mask on a pole, draped in a long robe: here is another link between Dionysus and the Greek theatre. The actors also become another person, and they wear a mask. Dionysus was in addition a god associated with disguise and illusion, with being transformed from one person or state to another, as happens in the theatre. These complex and varied forms which Dionysus adopted and represented were an important element in the close links between him and the theatre.

Drama and religion

Drama and religion have also had close connections in other countries and civilisations – though in very varied ways, since the celebration of religion has itself taken many different forms. In some traditions a dramatic event is a central part of the cult or worship. Obvious examples here are the Eucharistic sacrament of the bread and wine in Christian churches, or the ceremony of baptism. Religious drama was common in the medieval period, with the cycles of Mystery Plays in England. Right up to the twentieth century religious plays have continued to be a common form of theatrical portrayal. However, it is clear that for most people, most of the time, the link between religion and the theatre has weakened (as, indeed, it gradually did even in ancient Greece) and is considered an irrelevance for most theatrical viewing. Of course, part of the religious aspect was the mass congregation of people for a regular ritual celebration. In our societies that function is performed far more often by 'secular' events – attendance at a football match being perhaps the most obvious modern example: it is not a coincidence that lyrical football commentators often resort to the metaphor of the theatre to convey the event – 'this great drama in two acts'; 'the protagonists [from the Greek for 'leading actor'] locked in conflict'; 'the ebb and flow of human emotion, leading ultimately to *catharsis*' (see page 39); 'the dramatic dénouement'. It is possible, indeed, that the behaviour of a football crowd in some ways gives a far closer approximation to that of some 15,000 people packed together in the bowl of the theatre of Dionysus, on the slopes of the Acropolis in Athens, than does that of a few hundred genteel figures, slumped in their soft-upholstered seats in a plush indoor theatre in a modern city. That is to say, going to the theatre for a Greek was a collective experience; today it is for each individual member of the audience a private, solitary one – though (as any actor knows) the corporate mood of the audience can still be a powerful part of that experience and we all, perhaps, hope to find ourselves caught up in that mood.

The kinds of Greek play

The importance of the religious associations and the link with Dionysus can be examined by looking at the three different types of play which were performed: **satyr-plays**, **tragedies** and **comedies**.

SATYR-PLAYS

We know much less about these than the other main kinds of play, but evidently they were a very important part of the Greek theatre, and were probably the earliest plays of all. They took their name from the chorus of *satyrs*. These satyrs were strange, wild male creatures in Greek legend, often associated closely with the female nymphs: they formed the original revel band of Dionysus. They often behaved like beasts, and in Greek art they are most frequently represented as having animal features – with snub noses, pointed ears and horses' tails. They were often linked with other legendary creatures called the *Silenoi*. One satyr-play which survives today is *Cyclops* by Euripides. It tells the famous story (adapted from Homer's epic tale, the *Odyssey*) of how Odysseus blinded the one-eyed giant Polyphemus. In the play the chorus of Silenoi, under their leader Silenos, have a large role, although they are not mentioned in Homer's version of the story. Silenos is often represented in Greek art; Figure 4 shows one representation of him in ancient sculpture, though without the animal characteristics often evident on vase-paintings. In legend he and the rest of the Silenoi became the followers of Dionysus, and they are often to be found making or drinking the wine associated with that god.

TRAGEDIES

The word 'tragedy' is familiar in English. We use it rather generally to refer to any disaster or misfortune: the word 'tragic', which is connected with 'tragedy', means 'sad' and, like that word, it has become somewhat debased in everyday usage. For the Greeks 'tragedy' referred specifically to a play of a particular kind. Scholars have debated for many years the reason what the word 'tragedy' (*tragodia* in its Greek form) meant and why it was used for these plays. It may have meant, originally, 'goat-song', perhaps because the original chorus dressed in goatskins or competed at the festival, as some think, for the prize of a goat; others believe the word may have been somehow connected with wine. In either case, there was undoubtedly a strong link between tragedy and the cult of Dionysus, just as there was in the case of the satyr-plays.

4. *Silenos*

COMEDIES

The word 'comedy' is also a familiar one. It denotes, especially, something which is meant to make us laugh, and also comes from a Greek word (*comodia*) which means 'the song of the merrymakers (revellers)'. These revellers behaved and sang in a happy, festive manner, so the word has not greatly changed its fundamental meaning. Fancy dress was a common feature of the revels (see Figs. 1, p. 4 and 18, p. 42). The revellers accompanied processions at the beginning of the festivals of Dionysus, in the *komos* (celebratory revel). They welcomed the god's arrival in the city, singing and dancing in high spirits.

The first actors

All three types of play, then, developed from the worship of Dionysus and they included choruses who sang and danced in honour of the god. They first performed the *dithyramb*, a poetic composition sung by choruses of fifty men or boys. Dithyrambic competitions remained an important element in the Festival of Dionysus, giving large numbers of people the opportunity to participate. However, if there had only been such choruses, the theatre would never have developed into what we recognise today, since there would have been no actors – for us an essential requirement in a play.

Thespis

One man, Thespis, is especially associated with the birth of the theatre and his name is still commemorated today, when actors are sometimes called 'thespians'. Thespis is often regarded as the true founder of the theatre. The tradition is that he won the prize when tragedy was first performed at the Great Dionysia, around 534 BC. At this time it seems that tragic performances were already part of the festival, but probably in a quite different form from the tragedies which developed later. Thespis himself is said to have been the leader of the chorus, and to have taken a 'dramatic' step by turning round to face the chorus and holding conversations with them, while *impersonating* a *character* from the story being portrayed in their song. He may also have spoken a prologue to the audience, explaining what was going to happen. The Greek word for actor was *hypocrites* ('answerer') and to us a 'hypocrite' is a kind of actor: someone who pretends to be something else.

Aeschylus

The next substantial change came with the playwright Aeschylus (Fig. 5). He introduced a second actor. Before this, the single actor spoke only to the chorus; but now two actors could speak to each other and were therefore able to present scenes which did not necessarily involve the chorus. This gave playwrights much more freedom and scope for creating characters.

Sophocles

The second playwright Sophocles (Fig. 6) went one step further than Aeschylus by introducing a third actor. In the Greek theatre of the fifth century BC there were never more than three actors, although it was possible for more than three *characters* to appear in a play, provided that not all were on stage at the same time. All that the actor had to do was to change costume and mask, in order to become a new character. The chorus-leader continued to join in the dialogue and there were often silent 'extras' as well.

Nobody really knows why there was this limit of three actors. However, in the early days of the theatre there were no professionals making their living from it, as actors do today. Actors had to be trained specially for the festival, so that for the producer/director it was perhaps more manageable to work with a small number.

5. *Aeschylus (526-456 BC)*

Euripides

Figure 7 portrays Euripides, the last of the three great writers of Greek tragedy whose works have survived to the present day. Euripides was about ten years younger than Sophocles, but they often competed against each other in the Festival of the Great Dionysia. Although Euripides made innovations in the style and performance of tragedy, he did not introduce any actors beyond the limit of three.

Each of this trio of writers composed many plays which have not survived until today, but those which exist are listed in Appendix I. We have nineteen plays by Euripides, compared with only seven by each of Aeschylus and Sophocles.

6. *Sophocles (496-406 BC)*

7. *Euripides (485-406 BC)*

2
The festival of the Great Dionysia

The main festival at which plays were performed was the Great Dionysia, held in Athens in March every year. This chapter aims to answer a number of basic questions about the event. What did the theatre look like? How was the festival organised and what were its purposes? What form did the theatrical competitions take? Who came to see the performances? Who produced the plays and how were they paid for?

In trying to understand the answers to such questions, we must go back to Athens in the year 442 BC when, according to scholars, one of Sophocles' most famous plays, *Antigone*, was first performed. This section imagines the preparations for the performance.

The theatre of Dionysus

The oldest theatre in Greece is that of Dionysus at Athens and here *Antigone* received its first performance. The theatre was part of the area (or 'precinct') dedicated to the god Dionysus, which included temples and shrines set up in his honour. It was on the slopes of the *Acropolis*, a prominent hill in the centre of Athens. On the Acropolis still stands the famous temple in honour of the city's patron goddess, Athene: this is the Parthenon and it was built in the fifth century BC, at very much the time when Sophocles was writing plays such as *Antigone*. The Acropolis rises steeply from the plains below, and the Athenians had originally used it as a defence against invaders. In 442 BC, it was the religious centre of the city, as well as being close to its political heart, and it provided a natural site for the first theatre.

The Greeks always built their theatres in the open air. The builders used the natural curve of hillsides for the seating area. One reason for this was that they discovered that such sites often provided superb acoustics, which designers ever since have envied. Right from the back of the huge theatres every sound is clearly audible.

The theatre of Dionysus, like other Greek theatres, can still be visited but it has changed since the days of Sophocles, especially as the result of modifications in Roman times. A recent photograph (see Fig. 12) shows how it looks now. To see what it was like when *Antigone* was first performed, we need to take away the later additions, as on the plan shown in Figure 8.

The spectators' seats are in a curving area, a little more than a semi-circle, and slope down to the centre. The Greeks called this the *theatron* ('watching-place') from which our word 'theatre' comes. At the time of the first production of *Antigone*, the seats were probably wooden, but soon afterwards stone ones were built. It is generally estimated that between 14,000 and 17,000 people crowded in for the performances. The complete circle (shown

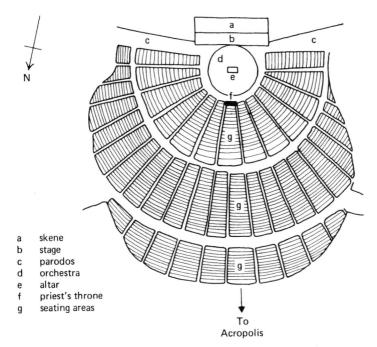

N

a	skene
b	stage
c	parodos
d	orchestra
e	altar
f	priest's throne
g	seating areas

To
Acropolis

8. *Plan of the theatre of Dionysus*

on the plan) in the middle of the seating area is the *orchestra* – this Greek word has also come into our language with a change of meaning. It was the dancing-place, where the chorus performed their songs and dances and were often joined by the actors. In the centre of the *orchestra* there was an altar to Dionysus, a reminder that the theatre was dedicated to him; sometimes the plots of the plays contained religious ceremonies which were performed at this altar.

To the rear was the *skene* (stage-building), from which the English word 'scene' comes. This was a wooden building where actors could change, and it also served as the background for the play, as a house, a temple or a palace. The front wall of the *skene* had a large double door which opened for actors to make their entrances, and there were probably two smaller doors as well, one on each side. The action of the play always took place out of doors, unlike that of most modern productions.

In front of the stage-building there was a low, wooden platform or stage, on which actors could stand, with steps leading down to the *orchestra*. From this, the actors could easily speak with the chorus. Actors entered the theatre either from the stage-building, as mentioned above, or from a *parodos* (side-entrance) if they were representing characters who were arriving from another town or country. There were two of these side-entrances, one on each side of the *orchestra*, and the chorus made its entry from one of these.

The theatre had three possible levels for actors to use: the platform in front of the stage-building; the *orchestra* where they could mingle with the chorus; and the roof of the stage-building – which could be reached by steps from inside and tended to be reserved for special moments or appearances.

The *choregos*, or sponsor

Apart from the playwright, the most important person concerned with the preparations for the dramatic competitions at the festival was the *choregos*, or sponsor. Because the festival was such an important part of the Athenians' life and of their state and religious calendar, the duty of sponsoring the plays was seen as an honourable and prestigious one for some of the richest of the citizens, who were all male. We shall be looking at the tasks of the sponsor who collaborated with Sophocles on the production of *Antigone* in 442 BC. Although we do not really know his name, we shall call him Bion, the name of a sponsor who, we know, worked with Sophocles a few years earlier.

The appointment of the sponsors

Each new year in Athens, a fresh set of officials took up their positions to supervise the political life of the city for the coming year. Among these were ten men appointed to the position of *archon* (senior magistrate), and the leading *archon* was in charge of the Great Dionysia, one of his functions being to select six sponsors from among the wealthy citizens. Such citizens had to help the city by undertaking certain public duties as a kind of tax on their wealth: these were called 'liturgies'. When Bion was appointed as *choregos*, he could also have been asked to perform other duties of this kind, such as paying for the equipment of a warship. Like others of his class, however, he would have been expected to welcome the opportunity afforded by such an appointment to help his city and to display his wealth in a good cause. There were three sponsors such as Bion for the tragic competition (one for each playwright selected to take part), and three for the comic plays. Lots were drawn to decide which sponsor was to work with which playwright. This method of selection by lot was characteristic of many Athenian institutions, since it represented the idea of fairness.

The duties of the sponsors

Bion's main duties as a sponsor were concerned with the chorus. This was a group of fifteen men, all Athenian citizens, who had to be trained to learn the words, music and dances which formed such a central part of the plays. The performance of the chorus was very important when the plays were judged in the competition, so the quality of their training was vital to a good production.

Each tragic playwright had one day on which to present four plays. There were three tragedies and then a satyr-play, performed one after the other. This meant that the chorus had to learn four sets of words, and wear four different costumes. Bion had to find the money for all of these.

Bion was, therefore, the financial backer. He had to pay the wages of the chorus and hire the musician who accompanied them on the reed instrument, the *aulos*, which was rather like a double oboe. Any special effects of scenery had to be paid for as well. There were not many of these, compared with modern theatres, but, since Sophocles was renowned for the introduction of *skene*-painting, he may have wanted a specially painted background for *Antigone*.

Bion did not train the chorus himself. Sophocles, as it happened, was an expert on the art of the chorus (he even wrote a book about it); he had also acted in some of his own plays but had retired from acting by now because, by the age of 55, he had had trouble with his voice on stage. Without Sophocles to train his chorus Bion would have had to hire an expert trainer.

The actors

The sponsor had no say in the selection or training of the three actors but he will have taken a keen interest in their progress: in several scenes the chorus and actors worked closely together. A few years earlier, in 449 BC, the Athenians had introduced a prize for the best actor, for which only the three *protagonists* (leading actors) – one for each playwright – were eligible. This was added to the existing prize for the best playwright, and it no doubt helped to make the competition even keener. Good actors could help a poor play greatly, while bad actors could ruin an excellent one.

The magistrate drew lots to decide which of the three chosen leading actors would perform for which of the three tragic playwrights. So although the leading actor had a principal role in each of his four plays, Sophocles and Bion had absolutely no control over this important decision. However, Sophocles could choose his own *deuteragonist* (second actor) and *tritagonist* (third actor). We know that the leading actor for Sophocles on at least one occasion was called Heracleides. And Sophocles himself often chose Tlepolemos to act for him, while another actor called Dicaiarchos also used to appear in his plays. We shall therefore use these names for the three actors who performed for Sophocles in 442 BC.

Costumes

Costumes were extremely important in enabling the actors to show the audience what character they were playing. It is not clear exactly what costumes were like in Sophocles' day, since (like the theatres) they changed later. But we can look at helpful illustrations from vases painted not long after *Antigone* was written. One of these (Fig. 18 p. 42) is a painting of women worshipping Dionysus. The god is in the centre, represented by a pillar covered by a mask and a decorated robe, with a long pleated skirt underneath. Another vase painting (Fig. 9) shows an actor wearing a highly decorated outfit and holding a mask. He is actually preparing for a satyr-play but the tragic costume was evidently much like this.

The tragic actor's costume consisted, it seems, of a full-length robe which could be covered by a shorter cloak, falling to below knee-length; the sleeves were long, tight and often patterned, and designs might include various decorations such as stripes, spirals or animal shapes. Actors who were playing the part of poor men or women would wear much plainer clothes than those for kings or heroes, and characters in mourning always wore black robes. The tragic mask, which was always worn, together with soft leather boots made up the complete costume. These boots were not the high 'platform' style which is often shown in modern representations of the Greek theatre; those belong, rather, to the Roman theatre which followed.

The style of costume made it far easier for men to take women's parts, which they had to do as there were no actresses in the Greek theatre. (The same was true in Shakespeare's time.) Arms and legs were hidden, and a female mask completed the disguise.

Masks

At the time of the first performance of *Antigone*, tragic masks looked quite natural, like those in Figures 9 and 10. To make it easier for all the audience to see actors' faces, the eyes and the mouth were slightly exaggerated and the mask, which fitted over the whole head, was rather larger than life. Masks were usually made of linen but sometimes cork or wood was used. The masks had lifelike hair, long or short and of various colours. An opening in the mouth made it possible for the actors to be heard clearly, with the help of the theatre's excellent natural acoustics. There were also eyeholes to enable them to see.

Greeks did not expect actors to imitate people in real life as we do, but the masks and costumes still had to allow them to move and speak easily and clearly. They also made it possible for the audience to distinguish one character from another from the back of the theatre: there were no opera glasses in those days.

9. *The actor's costume*

Masks present actors with one difficulty, of course – they cannot show feelings by using the expressions on their faces. In films or television plays close-up shots can show what a character is supposed to be feeling without any words or movement. Masked actors cannot demonstrate by facial expression laughter or crying, or emotions such as astonishment or horror. Apart from their own gestures and movements, they must rely on their tone of voice and the words of the play. Greek audiences were accustomed to using their imagination, and did not expect the kind of realism found in modern drama.

10. *An actor with his mask*

Advertising the plays

Ancient Greece lacked the modern forms of advertising by which we find out what events are about to happen. However, Athens was a small city by our standards. In addition, the preparations took place out-of-doors, as there were no suitable indoor halls. Rehearsals were probably public occasions, with opportunities for passers-by to watch the actors and chorus at work. Rival sponsors may have had their spies out. What was Sophocles planning this year? In Athens news spread fast and the playwrights did not lack publicity, especially as the festivals were such a central feature of public life.

Just before the festival began, a special occasion took place at which Sophocles and Bion, together with their rivals, gave people an idea of what to expect. Each playwright brought along his actors, who were not wearing their costumes or masks but had garlands to suit the festival atmosphere. This was the time when the assembled crowds learned about the subjects of the plays.

The audience

The people took a great interest in preparations for the festival and the theatre was packed for performances, since the dramatic festival was such an important part of the calendar for the Athenians.

The large majority of those who watched the plays were Athenian citizens – rich and poor, the well-educated as well as those who could scarcely read or write. All citizens were men who were born as sons of existing citizens. There were also people living in Athens who came from other parts of Greece, and many visitors came especially for the festival, sometimes making their first sea voyage of the new season, since the seas had been 'closed' in the winter. Young men and boys who were not yet full adult citizens attended the plays. There has been great debate as to whether women were present – and this still continues. There are references in some plays which may suggest that there were a few women spectators, but this is really not certain. Slaves were probably not allowed to attend, except for a few who acted as public officials.

There was fierce competition for seats. Entry was by ticket and the number admitted was controlled by how many were issued. Many tickets, made of ivory, lead or bone, have been discovered. They did not have a seat number but indicated which block of seating the ticket-holder was to sit in. Individual seats could not be numbered in a theatre of this kind but the seating area was divided into a number of wedge-shaped blocks. The ten tribes of Athenian citizens all had their own blocks and there were special seats at the front of the theatre for important people. One belonged to the priest of Dionysus, who sat in the front row. In one comedy (*The Frogs*, by Aristophanes), an actor playing the god Dionysus came right across the *orchestra* and appealed to the priest to rescue him from danger. He promised to buy him a drink after the show if he helped him! The priest's throne is shown in Figure 11. The Greek inscription can be made out clearly, singling it out as the seat of the priest (ΙΕΡΕΩΣ) of Dionysus (ΔΙΟΝΥΣΟΥ). In addition, there was a reserved block of seats for the 500 members of the Council (*Boule*), a representative group of Athenian citizens, once again selected each year by lot, who prepared the conduct of the city's democratic business.

We do not know how people obtained tickets but the price was two *obols*. This was a small sum but, even so, any poor citizens who applied to the authorities for a ticket were admitted free. The authorities then paid the fee to the official in charge of the theatre buildings. The fact that there was a special fund of money (the *Theoric Fund*) for this purpose underlines the importance which the Athenians attached to attendance at the theatre as a civic duty.

As the festival approached, excitement rose. The atmosphere must have been rather like that on an important sporting occasion today, as the visitors streamed in from all over the place towards the large open-air arena. This was an event which happened only once a year and, for visitors from other cities, perhaps only once in a lifetime.

11. *The throne of the priest of Dionysus*

The start of the festival

After all the preparations, the opening of the festival arrived. It was an event marked by celebrations of the city of Athens and its achievements. The festival began with a great procession; sacrifices were offered to Dionysus, including the bull which was led in the procession. The scene was very colourful, with a variety of sacred objects and offerings, especially a golden basket carried by a young girl of noble birth. Bion and the other sponsors dressed in magnificent gowns and many other visitors wore brightly-coloured clothes. Even those who had not obtained theatre tickets took part in the festival as the procession made its noisy, merry way through the streets.

After the sacrifices came the first competitions. These did not include any actors, but large numbers of men and boys took part in choral recitations and dancing. The first evening was time for the *komos* (revel), when lively singing and dancing in honour of Dionysus carried on late into the night.

12. *The theatre of Dionysus, Athens*

The acting competitions

The next three days were devoted to the plays. Before the first play came important ceremonies: the generals (*strategoi*) appeared in person, there were parades of young men and announcements were made to honour citizens who had served the state well. By this time, no doubt, Bion and Sophocles felt that they had done all they could and could only wait, while taking a full part in the ceremonies as proud Athenian citizens. Final rehearsals had been held. Everyone, it was hoped, knew the words and the dances. No expense had been spared with the costumes and masks for the chorus and actors. Bion had encouraged his friends to attend and cheer for Sophocles. This was his only chance of success with the plays written for this year's festival, including *Antigone*. After this one performance there was no possibility of a long run, as there is for a new play in London's West End or New York's Broadway. The following year – win or lose – Sophocles would be back, if he was selected, with four new plays.

At the time of Sophocles, the pattern, after the opening day's ceremonials, was as follows:

The second day: The first tragic playwright produced his four plays – three tragedies and a satyr-play. These began early in the morning and went on, with short breaks, for perhaps six hours. Then there was an interval, when people ate their lunches, which they usually brought with them (though snacks were also on sale in the theatre). Afterwards, there was a single comedy, by the first of the comic playwrights. The order of playwrights was decided by drawing lots.

The third day: The second tragic writer and comic writer produced their plays, in the same order.

The fourth day: The third and final group of five plays was presented.

The fifth day: The judging of the best playwright and actor in each section, comedy and tragedy, took place and the prizes were presented.

It may seem amazing to us that audiences sat on uncomfortable seats through a total of fifteen plays in three days. Of course, some people today spend many hours each day watching television from the comfort of their armchairs. For the Greeks, however, this was something quite different, because of the great importance which the festival occupied in the life of Athens. Something of the same fervour is no doubt experienced by the devotees of the operas of Wagner who flock to the Bayreuth Festival to see performances of the Ring cycle, or to such pop festivals as that held at Glastonbury.

The day of judgement

If Sophocles had his plays performed on the festival's second day, then he, Bion, the actors and chorus had two full days afterwards to watch the entries of the other two tragic playwrights and enjoy the light relief offered by the comedies towards evening. And then the festival approached its climax.

Beforehand a list of a hundred names had been drawn up, ten from each tribe of Athenian citizens, from which the judges were to be selected. Each tribe had been given an urn into which tablets bearing the ten names were placed; these were not to be interfered with. The names were those of ordinary Athenians – the judges were not expected to be experts.

Just before the first play began, the magistrate drew out one name from each urn and the ten men who were selected by lot in this way (one from each tribe) swore solemnly that they would judge fairly. On the fifth day, after all the plays had been presented, each judge wrote on another tablet his order of merit for the three tragic playwrights, of whom in 442 BC Sophocles was one, and the ten tablets were again placed in an urn. Five were drawn out, in order to ensure that there was little possibility of cheating, and the writer who had the most votes in first place was declared the winner. The actors' competition was also judged, probably in a similar way.

Despite all these elaborate precautions we know that there were attempts to influence the judging. A sponsor might on occasion attempt to bribe the judges, or to have his friends entered on the original list. Sometimes trials were held after the festival to investigate incidents of this kind. The judges themselves did not have to explain why they voted as they did, but simply had to choose which playwright they liked best. The system was certainly a

13. *Masks for the Greek theatre. Mask (a) is for a young girl, like Antigone; and mask (b) shows a king, like Agamemnon or Oedipus. The others are for satyr-plays or comedies: compare mask (c) with the picture of Silenos on p. 9*

careful one. Even if not perfect, it enabled Sophocles to win eighteen times; this surely gives some indication of the quality of the judging. It was a democratic system, as we might expect in Athens, the city which founded democracy. It meant that ordinary people were closely involved in the festival. In fact, with all the actors, members of choruses, judges and magistrates, a substantial number of the 40,000 or so Athenian citizens took some part in events.

The end of the festival

After the judging came the prize-giving ceremonies, when the winning playwright and actor were presented with a wreath and a prize of money – we do not know how much. In 442 BC it seems that Sophocles won the playwrights' competition; one story is that, because of the popularity which *Antigone* brought him, he was appointed to the very important political post of general (*strategos*) the following year. He was quite a well-to-do man, like many of the playwrights, and the money mattered less than the prestige. For the successful leading actor there was an automatic opportunity to act in the following year's festival, while the sponsor who had financed the winning plays could set up a monument to record his victory. Some of these still stand today and provide a further important source of evidence about the history of the Greek theatre.

When the festival had finished, the Athenian citizens held an assembly (*ekklesia*), and carefully examined the way in which the magistrate had organised everything: if they disapproved, he could be fined. And then it was all over. Citizens went back to work, playwrights no doubt started thinking about what they would write for next year's competition. Not all of the scripts would have been preserved, but some were – especially those by Aeschylus, Sophocles and Euripides; and they were therefore available to be revived, as they were during the next century, a practice which helped to keep them alive for later generations.

3
The first performance of Antigone

Choice of subject

Unlike modern writers, Sophocles did not have a completely free hand in his choice of subject matter. Practically all tragedies dealt with Greek myths and legends. (There is only one real exception among surviving plays – *The Persians*, by Aeschylus, which describes the victory of the Greeks over King Xerxes of Persia.)

Some explanations can be offered for why the writers kept using the same themes. Firstly, the Greeks took stories of their early heroes far more seriously than we take legends such as 'King Arthur and the Knights of the Round Table' or 'Robin Hood', although these too are often used in plays and films. The Greeks learned Homer's poems, the *Iliad* and the *Odyssey*, from a very early age and many Athenians could quote long sections from them. The heroes of the poems, the legendary figures of the Trojan War (Achilles, Agamemnon, Odysseus and others), often feature in the tragedies. Other plays have heroes from the royal houses of such Greek cities as Mycenae and Thebes; according to the legends, both houses suffered terrible disasters.

Secondly, the festivals were, as we have seen, religious occasions. The Greeks believed that the gods had once mingled freely with mortals and they often feature in the plays. These legendary stories were therefore not simply fairy tales. Questions about religion and morality often occurred in the legends, and the playwrights explored these questions. How should people act towards the gods and towards each other? Should one murder always be avenged by another? Issues of this kind constantly concerned the tragic playwrights. They were also, importantly, often the topics which concerned the people in the democracy of Athens and this shows again the close link between the religious and civic or political aspects of the theatre. The use of myth, it has been suggested, provided a way of dealing with difficult contemporary issues from a relatively 'safe' perspective.

The Greeks did not think playwrights were unoriginal if they dealt with a familiar story. Instead, they doubtless admired the ways in which the playwrights could use the same stories to express different ideas. All three of the great tragic writers – Aeschylus, Sophocles and Euripides – wrote plays about Electra and Orestes, the daughter and son of Agamemnon and Clytemnestra (the king and queen of Mycenae). These three plays told the story of how

Electra and Orestes planned to murder their mother because she had killed Agamemnon on his return from Troy. But the plays are very different from one another.

The choice of Antigone, daughter of Oedipus (the legendary king of Thebes), was in line with Sophocles' usual subjects; two of his other surviving plays also deal with Oedipus and Thebes. It was not, therefore, the story which made Sophocles' play original but the way he treated it.

The play's background

When King Oedipus learnt that he had killed his father and married his mother (without realising what he had done), he blinded himself and gave up the throne of Thebes. He went into exile. His brother-in-law, Creon, ruled the city until Oedipus' two sons were old enough to reign. When they grew up the sons quarrelled over which should be king, and the younger led an army against the city of Thebes. To settle the dispute seven men were chosen from each side, including the two brothers. They had to fight each other in single combat. In the critical battle the brothers killed each other, leaving Creon as king. The invading army retreated from Thebes.

The legend was familiar to many of the audience, although others, especially some of the visitors to Athens, may have known no more than the title of the play. There were no programme notes to tell them who the characters or actors were. However, unlike the audience, we are in a position to look at a list of the characters of *Antigone.*

The characters

Antigone ⎫	daughters of Oedipus
Ismene ⎭	
Creon	king of Thebes
Eurydice	his wife, the queen
Haimon	son of Creon and Eurydice
Teiresias	a blind prophet
Guard	
Messenger	
Chorus	respected Theban citizens
Extras:	soldiers, servants, boy leading Teiresias

The first striking thing about this list is that there are eight speaking parts to be played by three actors; also it is noticeable that three characters are female. We have seen that costumes and masks made things easier but, even so, the actors clearly had many difficult challenges. They had to be able to change their voices and acting styles convincingly to create new characters; hence the best actors were highly sought-after by writers such as Sophocles.

The same actor, of course, could not play two characters who were on stage at the same time but this still leaves several possible combinations. Though we cannot be certain, the following arrangement works well:

Heracleides (*protagonist*): Creon
Tlepolemos (*deuteragonist*): Antigone, Haimon, and Messenger
Dicaiarchos (*tritagonist*): Ismene, Guard, Teiresias, and Eurydice

The demands on the actors

Heracleides, as Creon, has only one role to play, but it is a very long part. He enters early and is involved in the action until the final scene. Tlepolemos has one long, important woman's role – perhaps Sophocles chose him with this in mind. He also has to deliver two important messenger speeches. Although Haimon and Antigone are to marry they never appear on stage at the same time, so the same actor can play both parts. This underlines the limitations which the number of actors inevitably imposed on Sophocles and also the different expectations of the Greeks: it is hard to imagine a modern playwright not wishing to make more of the 'romantic' interest, by having at least one scene involving the two young lovers. Dicaiarchos has several quick changes of character. At one moment he is a princess, then a guard; later he becomes an old prophet and finally he is the queen of Thebes. Perhaps on the night before the performance, while Heracleides and Tlepolemos are going over their big speeches to make sure of their words, Dicaiarchos is trying out his different costumes and voices. In the performance he will need expert assistance from a back-stage crew, who help him with his rapid changes of costume. A late entry would be disastrous.

The three actors and crew arrive early on the day of the performance and enter the stage-building (*skene*) by the back door. Figure 14 shows the stage-building, where the actors wait for their entries and change costumes and masks. The man who operates the *mechane* (a kind of crane which can raise characters above the level of the stage and enable them to fly across it) is not needed for *Antigone*, but several other plays in the competition may well require his skill. The other piece of equipment which is shown, the *ekkyklema*, is a trolley which can be wheeled through the central doors. This is used in *Antigone*, and two men are needed to wheel it into position.

The drawing also shows the three acting levels. The roof of the *skene*, which is reached by steps from inside the building, can represent a palace roof – as in *Agamemnon*, a play by Aeschylus. In a number of productions, gods make appearances from this roof, as if they are speaking from the heavens.

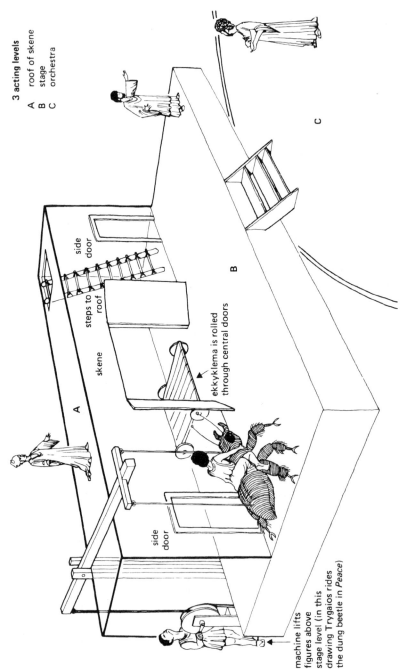

3 acting levels

A roof of skene
B stage
C orchestra

side door

steps to roof

skene

A

side door

ekkyklema is rolled through central doors

B

C

machine lifts figures above stage level (in this drawing Trygaios rides the dung beetle in *Peace*)

14. *The stage and stage-building* (skene), *showing the* **mechane** *and* **ekkyklema**, *and the three acting levels*

The play begins

We are now ready for the start of the play – and so is the audience. From the earliest glimpse of light they have been flocking to the theatre of Dionysus and are now crammed together in the seating area, looking down at the bare *orchestra*. They are all waiting for the blast of the trumpet which will announce the start of the competition. We shall imagine that *Antigone* is the first of the fifteen they will see.

The judges are sworn in. Out of sight in the *skene*-building Tlepolemos and Dicaiarchos check their costumes for their first entrance. Sophocles and Bion are giving the cast last-minute words of encouragement: they do not stay in the *skene* during the performance. They will become involved only if there are problems with the production; and it is, of course, the only opportunity which they will have to see the play performed to an audience. The musician who accompanies the chorus on the *aulos* gently runs through the tunes. He does not want the audience to hear him, but he need not worry: the excited chatter drowns out any sound from his instrument.

The trumpet sounds and a sudden hush comes over the audience. As they look towards the *skene*, the double doors in the centre swing open. A solitary figure in female clothing emerges, followed, after a short pause, by another. The first few words tell the audience that the second girl is called Ismene, and soon her sister Antigone is also introduced by name. If the audience does not understand the background to the play, it may prove difficult to follow the thread of the plot. Antigone tells Ismene why she has brought her outside the palace, putting the audience in the picture at the same time.

> ANTIGONE: I have asked you to come outside so that I can tell you something, without anyone overhearing.
> ISMENE: What is it, Antigone? I see you have bad news for me.
> ANTIGONE: Ismene, do you not know that King Creon has given orders for one of our brothers to be buried, and not the other? Eteocles has had a fine funeral, I hear, but Polyneices, so Creon says, must receive neither burial nor mourning. His body must be left unwept, to be a feast for vultures...
> Now you must show whether you are really a king's daughter, or not.
> ISMENE: Antigone, what can I do? How can I help you?...
> ANTIGONE: You can help me bury Polyneices' corpse.
>
> [Sophocles, *Antigone* 18-30, 37-40, 43]

Ismene refuses and Antigone storms back into the palace, angry at her sister's unwillingness to disobey Creon. Ismene follows Antigone inside, anxious about her sister's well-being.

In the *skene* Tlepolemos and Dicaiarchos prepare for their next entries. Tlepolemos has to wait for some time for his second appearance as Antigone, but Dicaiarchos has a difficult change to make. He now has to become a down-to-earth peasant soldier, instead of a young princess. In the opening scene, the two actors have been able to show something of the characters of the sisters: Ismene is timid and obedient to orders; Antigone is defiant, passionate and domineering. The audience now has an idea what the play may be about. Will Antigone really disobey Creon's orders, and what will happen if she does?

The entry of the chorus

Once again the *orchestra* is empty and the palace doors are shut. Now from the right-hand side, out beyond the *skene,* are heard the strange, reedy notes of the musician. Dressed in splendid costume, he leads in the fifteen members of the chorus. With the quiet dignity of prominent Theban citizens they walk towards the rising sun, through the *parodos* and into the *orchestra*; they enter perhaps in three rows of five. The best performers are doubtless placed nearest to the audience, possibly with the next-best group at the back; any who are less experienced, or who are not quite such good dancers or singers, can be slightly hidden in between. All turn and face the audience to perform their opening number. They sing in unison, with a strong rhythmic pattern, accompanied by the musician. They act out their song with carefully re-hearsed movements.

It is a critical moment for Bion. A good opening chorus makes a great impact on the audience, and on the judges too. The members of the chorus take particular care over their words, which must rise above the music and be able to be heard throughout the theatre. They sing of the defeat of the invading army led by Polyneices, comparing him to an eagle swooping down on the city; they thank Zeus for delivering Thebes from the enemy. Their words give vital information to the audience, but the chorus also provides a pageant of colour, movement and music. It is difficult for us to imagine how the chorus looked and sounded, since there are no detailed records of their dances or music. To the Greeks the chorus was an integral part of the play – certainly no less important than the actors. The choral passages were anything but mere interludes to separate the acting scenes and give actors time to change their costumes; they were very much at the heart of the entire spectacle and action, and made a profound impression on their own. Figure 15, showing the chorus in a modern production, gives some idea of their striking appearance, but can hardly begin to suggest what a powerful element in the drama they constituted.

The entry of Creon

Creon enters (played by Heracleides). The chorus-leader (who is dressed more colourfully than the rest of the chorus) names the new arrival, so that the audience can be in no doubt. It is Heracleides' big moment and he goes

15. *Agamemnon's return from Troy. A scene from a modern performance of* Agamemnon *in Greek at the open-air theatre at Bradfield College*

straight into a long, important speech, telling the Thebans his decision about the two brothers:

> CREON: I have made the following proclamation about the two sons of Oedipus. Eteocles, who died fighting to defend his city, must receive all the honours due to those who die nobly. The other one (you know who I mean, his brother Polyneices), who returned from exile to destroy and set fire to his own land and turn his people into slaves, must not be buried or mourned by anyone. I forbid it... As long as I live, if I can help it, evil will never defeat good. But he who serves his country loyally will be honoured in life and in death.
>
> [*Antigone*, 192-204, 207-10]

Heracleides ends his long speech, glad not to have faltered. He has established in the audience's mind that Creon is a figure with strong views and a determination to be a strong ruler.

At this moment a soldier enters from the *parodos*. The audience knows that this means that he is arriving from some distance, otherwise he would have come from the *skene*, like the members of the royal family. This is one of the men who have been set to guard the body of Polyneices, on Creon's orders. The actor is again Dicaiarchos, who now looks and sounds very different from the quiet Ismene whom he played in the opening scene. He is a soldier, his manner and speech slightly rough. He is also very nervous: Creon has to order him to come out with his story which he is reluctant, for obvious reasons, to tell.

> GUARD: Well, this is how it is, sir. It's the corpse. Someone's gone and buried it and cleared off, after scattering dust all over the body.
> CREON: What do you say? Who has dared do such a thing?
> GUARD: Search me, guv. There wasn't a trace of a spade or shovel. And as the ground was hard and dry, well, there were no tracks, either.

> [*Antigone*, 245-52]

The guard finishes his story, insisting that neither his fellow-guards nor he knew anything about it. Creon dismisses him angrily, telling him to make sure he finds the culprit or it will be the worse for him. Then Creon turns and strides back into the palace. The guard hurriedly escapes, relieved to be alive.

The story unfolds

During all this the members of the chorus have been standing in the *orchestra*, facing the audience. When the guard has left they sing their next song, a hymn about the achievements of the human race – suggesting, perhaps, to the minds of the audience the kind of confident, dominating person that Creon is. They add a comment, however, which hints that there are limits to human potential, with a final line which perhaps suggests a less optimistic development to the story:

> In this world are many wonders,
> None more wonderful than man.
> He can sail the stormy ocean;
> Through the deep his way he'll plan.
> Mother Earth to him must offer
> Year by year her rich supply.
> As he toils with beasts of burden,
> Nothing can his will deny.

All that lives on earth or heaven,
All that dwells beneath the sea,
He can capture with his cunning.
Nothing from his grasp can flee.
On the mountainside he chases,
Hunting lions to their den.
Horse and cattle learn to heed him.
All accept the rule of men.

Man has learnt the gift of language;
Fast as wind his speed of thought.
Shelters, houses, towns and cities,
All by man's great skill are wrought.
His the power that knows no limit;
His the cure for every ill.
He has conquered every danger.
Death alone defeats us still.

[*Antigone*, 332-62]

After this song, the guard returns – which is a surprise to the audience since he left swearing never to come back. With him, guarded by two soldiers, is Antigone. Most of the audience will no doubt have realised that it was Antigone who had covered Polyneices' body with dust, because they (unlike Creon, of course) have heard her words in the opening scene. However, they may be surprised to discover that she has now been caught as she appeared to have got away with it.

Creon is fetched from the palace, and for the first time all three actors are on stage together. A vase painting (Fig. 16) pictures this moment. First, the guard explains, vividly, why he has returned:

> GUARD: We swept away the dust from the body, and the corpse lay there again, all bare and wet. Then we sat down on the hill, getting as far away from the stinking flesh as possible. The stench was something terrible. We kept a pretty careful watch, I can tell you. We weren't going to be caught on the hop again. Well, some hours later, with the sun burning down from high in the sky, a duststorm sprang up, swept across the plain, tore the leaves off the trees and filled the sky. The only way to keep the dust out was to shut your eyes tight as you could. Then it stopped, and there she was. It was *her*, right enough – down by the body. She let out a wail, like a mother bird coming home to find her babies all gone from the nest, once she saw that the body was uncovered. Did she curse us! Then, she picks up the dust in her hands, and pours wine from a

bronze urn. That did it! We were down there like a shot, and we arrested her. We accused her of covering the body the first time too, and she admitted it.

Well, that puts me in the clear, I'm glad to say, but I'd rather not have landed her in the cart. I've got nothing against her. But it was a choice between her and me, you understand.

[*Antigone*, 402-40]

The guard has served his purpose and is dismissed again. There follows an angry scene between Creon and Antigone. For Creon, it is simple: the law is

16. *Antigone, Creon and the guard*

the law. For Antigone, it is equally simple: her brother was her brother and he had to be buried; that is the law of the dead.

Meanwhile, Dicaiarchos has done another hasty change and returns again as Ismene who, ashamed now that she has not helped Antigone, attempts to claim that she is also guilty. Antigone refuses her support. It is too late. Creon, despite his son's intended marriage to Antigone, is determined that she shall die. The law is the law. Antigone and Ismene are taken into the palace, leaving Creon alone with the chorus, who now sing about the disasters which have struck the house of Thebes.

Then Haimon enters, giving Tlepolemos his second role. There is a fierce argument (*agon*) between father and son. The Athenians were keen debaters, especially in the law-courts, and plays often contained a central debate such as this, which presented the main issues with which the play was concerned. Haimon's case is that the people of Thebes, not just Antigone, disagree with

Creon's decision not to bury Polyneices. Creon replies that he does not take orders from the people of Thebes. He refuses to pardon Antigone and Haimon departs, clearly very upset and angry. Then Creon announces the fate of Antigone: she is to be walled up in a cave with a little food. Creon believes that he will avoid bringing guilt or pollution on the city of Thebes if he does not kill her directly.

Shortly after, Antigone comes from the palace, guarded, and grieves for her fate. She was to have been escorted to her marriage but instead is to be led to her funeral. Creon again comes out, but not to pity her. He orders that she is to be taken at once to her rocky tomb, and Antigone, a sad figure, departs by the *parodos* on her last, long journey.

The climax approaches

The mood of the chorus is now very different from the earlier confident hymn. Their next dance is to a slow, sad rhythm and the music matches the mood. Creon still stands there, alone on the stage in front of the *skene*. While talking to Antigone and then to Haimon, he has shown no signs of pity or of willingness to yield. But now he has another test. This time he must face Teiresias, the old, blind prophet much respected by the people of Thebes. He enters from the *parodos*, led by a boy, and the slow pace of Antigone's farewell is mirrored by his gradual progress into the theatre. The boy is an 'extra' with no words to speak. It is a big day for him, too. Who knows? In a few years' time he may be the next Dicaiarchos. He listens and watches carefully as the experienced and versatile actor now adopts the movements and speech of an old man – an old man, but anything but weak. He represents a powerful threat to Creon, because prophets were dedicated to the gods and could be their mouthpiece. They demanded, and earned, the highest respect in Greek society.

Creon therefore greets Teiresias respectfully and listens to his words. They are not easy for him to bear. The prophet claims that it is Creon's fault that the sacrifices which he has been making have not been accepted by the gods. Creon, however, still refuses to change his mind; he thinks Teiresias is trying to deceive him, perhaps for money. After angry exchanges (see Fig. 17), Teiresias is led away by the boy. His parting words warn Creon that his own son Haimon will die.

Creon is finally affected. In his anxiety his mood changes and he begins to consult with the chorus-leader as to how he should act. Finally he accepts the advice that he should release Antigone, and hurries away. The chorus now sing a very joyful song, a hymn to Dionysus, god of revelry and of the theatre. The scene might well seem set for a happy ending. But then a messenger arrives, entering from the *parodos* by which both Antigone and Creon had left.

The messenger-speech

No death or violent action could take place on stage in Greek tragedy. The theatre was sacred to Dionysus and violent death polluted holy ground. Everything had to be conveyed to the audience in words and the device used

17. *Creon (kneeling) and the blind prophet Teiresias [from a production at Whitgift School]*

for this was normally a messenger arriving on the scene to deliver an eye-witness account. Such messenger-speeches are often among the most vivid moments of a play and can have an immensely powerful effect on the audience. To perform such a messenger-speech called for the actor's greatest skill; in *Antigone* Tlepolemos has to give two. He has just recovered from the difficult role of Antigone, for which he has had to adopt a strong female voice. Now he is a man again and must summon all his vocal powers for this speech. First he builds up the suspense, describing the scene as Creon, accompanied by his servants, approaches the rocky hill. Then he reaches the climax of his narrative; Creon, he says, has just heard a sound from inside the cave and is convinced that it is Haimon, his son:

> MESSENGER: There, right in the farthest corner of the cave, we saw her, hanging dead from a noose made from her own clothing. And there was Haimon, grieving for his dead bride, and for his

father's cruelty. Creon rushed to him, crying:

'Poor boy, what have you done? Why have you come here? I beg you, come away from this place. Come with me.'

But Haimon's eyes flashed with hatred, and he spat, full in his father's face. Then he drew a sword and struck out. Creon dodged the blow and fled, while Haimon, in a frenzy, thrust the sword deep in his own side. As the blood gushed from his mouth, he gave Antigone a final kiss, and the blood stained her white cheeks red. And so they lie, wedded in death, their bodies united.

[*Antigone*, 1220-40]

Eurydice, the queen, has listened to all of this in silence (a final part for Dicaiarchos), but before the end of the speech she goes into the palace. The messenger hurries after her and at this moment a sad procession appears from the *parodos*. Creon is leading the body of Haimon, borne by his servants, back home. At last he has learnt wisdom, but too late. 'The gods', he says, 'have destroyed my happiness'

Yet the final blow has still to fall. The messenger comes from the palace and delivers a second speech. Eurydice has taken her own life. The central doors are flung open and her body is brought out on the *ekkyklema* (see Fig. 14, p. 30). Creon can bear no more. He asks the gods to kill him too, but his punishment is to remain alive. Slaves lead him away, a broken man. The audience is completely silent. In the *orchestra* stand the members of the chorus, where they have been since their first entry. Now they turn quietly and leave. The final, brief words of the play, which they chant, sum up the play's message.

The greatest part of happiness is wisdom;
Divine laws man ought always to uphold.
To boastful tongues sure punishment will follow,
And wisdom we learn only when we're old.

[*Antigone*, 1347-53]

The play's effect

The effect on the audience can be imagined. They have followed with intense emotion the moods of the actors and chorus. They have wept and suffered with Antigone; her death (like the deaths of Haimon and Eurydice) has affected them deeply. The final sight they have witnessed has been the ruined Creon and they feel sympathy even for him, despite his earlier pride and cruelty.

A century after *Antigone* was first performed, the writer Aristotle used the word *catharsis* to try to explain the effect of tragedies. The word means 'cleansing' or 'purification': Aristotle believed that the intense emotions experienced by the spectators were somehow taken away at the end of watching a tragic play, as though these feelings – fear, joy, pity, suspense – had been washed away. Sometimes, even today, people may say that watching a play (or even a tense football match) has left them feeling 'drained'. While this may suggest slightly the state of the audience after watching the performance of *Antigone*, there was certainly more to it than that. Watching the play was part of a religious celebration for the Greeks. They were not mere spectators, but involved themselves deeply in the play and were seen, in a sense, to be part of the 'action' which was drama. At the end came a release of all the tension and passion. There was exhilaration as well as exhaustion.

To us perhaps the most astonishing thing of all is that after *Antigone*, with only a short pause, the same actors, chorus and audience embarked on a second tragedy, followed by a third, and then by the same writer's satyr-play. This was still closely linked to the tragedies in many ways, while representing a rather different approach and moving towards a triumphant celebration of the worship of Dionysus by his devoted followers. It was only after watching this quartet of plays by Sophocles, or one of his rivals, that the audience could really let their hair down by watching a comedy.

The theme of Antigone

Antigone was a play which made the audience think, as Sophocles undoubtedly intended. He raised questions which, while significant in particular ways to the Greeks, are just as important today. Should the law of the land always be obeyed? How should people act when their conscience clashes with the law? How should a state deal with someone who disobeys the law for reasons of individual conscience? Is Creon wrong to try to uphold the rule of law and stand by his decisions? Or is he wrong only to ignore advice or to treat people with arrogance, as he treated Antigone, Haimon and particularly Teiresias? Such questions may still be discussed today, and the discussions are surely not all that different from those which will have gone on in Athens at the time when Sophocles wrote *Antigone*.

4
Comedy in Greece

The Lenaia

The story of Greek comedy is, like that of tragedy, closely bound up with festivals to Dionysus. Comedy featured, as we have seen, at the Great Dionysia in Athens as an aftermath to the performances of tragedy and satyr-plays but another festival, the Lenaia, was especially devoted to comic plays. It was a winter festival, held each year in January and mainly attended by Athenians, from the city of Athens and surrounding countryside of Attica, because the seas were too stormy at that season to be safe for travel. In one comedy performed at the Lenaia a character states that 'there are no foreigners here yet...we are on our own' (Aristophanes, *The Acharnians*, 502-7). The Lenaia included some tragedies but not satyr-plays and it was with comedy that it was particularly associated. The great tragic playwrights, such as Sophocles, rarely presented their plays at this festival, where only two writers of tragedy competed, each with two plays. Five comic playwrights had their opportunity (except for a period late in the fifth century BC, when the war between Athens and Sparta reduced the number to three), each with a single play. As at the Great Dionysia, there were prizes for the best writer and actor, awarded both for tragedy and comedy. In the vase painting shown in Figure 18, the female worshippers of Dionysus, Bacchants or *maenads*, are shown celebrating the festival of the Lenaia.

An actor prepares for the Lenaia

The Lenaia is described in *The Mask of Apollo*, a novel by Mary Renault about the life of a Greek actor. In the following extract, a tragic actor tells how he prepares to take part:

> On the eve of the festival I lay listening to the noise of the midnight rites; the cries of the women trying, as they ran about the streets, to sound like *maenads* on a mountain. Their hymns, and their squeals of 'Iakchos' and the red light of torches sliding across the ceiling, would wake me whenever my eyes had closed. Towards morning, I heard a huddle of them go by with their torches out,

shivering and grumbling, and complaining of the rain.

Next day opened cloudy, not the rank bad weather that gets the show put off, but grey and threatening. During the first of the comedies it looked so black that the people stayed at home, and the theatre was half-empty; if the cast had been less discouraged, I think the play might have won...

18. *Dionysus and worshippers at the Lenaia, another festival of Dionysus*

On the day when the contest of the tragedies started, the wind got up. The audience came muffled to the eyes, their cloaks pulled over their heads, and with two cloaks if they had them...

The following day was ours.

I could not sleep. I thought of taking poppy-syrup; but it leaves one dull, and one would do better tired... I tossed and turned, and put my hand to the window, and felt the air still, but very cold... Suddenly I woke to daybreak. The lamp had burned out; birds were chirping. The sky was clear...

When we got to the theatre, the public benches were full of people bundled up in all they had, with hats pulled down on their ears. Down below, in the seats of honour, ambassadors and *archons* [officials], priests and *choregoi* with their guests were coming in, their slaves all laden with rugs and cushions to make them snug. Then came the greater priests and priestesses. Presently drums and cymbals sounded; the image of Dionysus was carried in and set down facing the *orchestra*, where he could see his servants play; his High Priest took the central throne; the trumpet sounded, and ceased...

[M. Renault, *The Mask of Apollo*]

Aristophanes and Old Comedy

The only surviving examples of Old Comedy (i.e. the comedies of the fifth century BC) were written by Aristophanes (see Appendix I). We have eleven of his plays and there are fragments or records of another thirty-two.

Aristophanes was evidently the most successful comic writer of his time but he was far from the only popular writer of comedies and he certainly did not always win first prize. Other comic playwrights, such as Cratinus, are known to us only from such small fragments that it is not really possible to judge their quality; Aristophanes sometimes makes unflattering references to them within his plays but, since he was trying to persuade the judges to vote for him, his views should not be regarded as totally objective. It is unfortunate that a lack of evidence makes it impossible to make the comparison for ourselves.

Aristophanes sometimes presented his plays at the Great Dionysia and sometimes at the Lenaia. It seems that he may have been more successful at the Lenaia since, in the absence of foreigners, he had greater freedom to put forward his ideas, which often included strong criticism and satire of the most prominent politicians of the day. His writing career stretched over forty years, starting in 427 BC. For most of this time Athens was engaged in a bitter war with its rival city-state, Sparta. Many of his plays were written and performed in wartime, and the subject of the war was hardly ever far from his mind. In January, however, fighting rarely took place because of the difficult weather conditions; the Lenaia was therefore held at a quiet time of the year. Aristophanes' plays usually took their titles from the chorus, which again underlines how important their function was. The surviving plays reveal what a variety of costumes the comic choruses must have had to wear over the years: *The Birds*, *The Frogs*, *The Clouds*, *The Wasps*. Figure 1 gives an idea of the kinds of costumes which would have been worn for *The Birds*, and the scene from a vase-painting (Fig. 19) shows a chorus of horsemen – perhaps rather as the chorus in *The Knights* might have appeared, though the painting is, in fact, almost a hundred years earlier than the play.

Acting in old comedy

There were similarities between acting in tragedy and in comedy. In each type of play there were only three actors who often had to play several parts, as we saw in *Antigone*. The rule about the three actors, however, was not applied quite so strictly in comedy and 'extras' could play minor speaking parts. As in tragedy, the actors in comedy wore masks and special costumes, and they relied greatly on the audience's powers of imagination: the same

simple theatre, with an *orchestra*, a simple stage and a *skene*-building, served
for both tragedy and comedy.

Despite these similarities, there were also important differences. There
was no doubt that comedies were meant to amuse and entertain their audiences. The actors, therefore, had to try all their tricks and skills – just as
stand-up comedians do today – to win the crowd over to their side. No doubt,

19. *A chorus of horsemen*

Greek actors also had to resist the temptation, if the laughs were not coming
as freely as they would have liked, to overact and strive too hard, with often
disastrous consequences. Today these difficulties are sometimes reduced for
television comedians by producers who indicate the desired response by
playing recorded laughter, or by inviting a studio audience, who are prompted
by flashing lights to applaud or laugh at the appropriate moment. In the theatre
there are still no automatic laughs and comic actors learn to their cost how
differently various audiences react.

It must have been particularly difficult for Aristophanes and his rivals. As
Mary Renault's novel *The Mask of Apollo* shows, their plays were presented
at the Lenaia to a cold, sometimes wet audience sitting in the open air on a
wintry day. However funny the play, everything depended on how well the
actors could put the humour – and also the more serious ideas – across to them.

Comic costumes

One of the most striking differences between the appearance of tragedy and
that of comedy was the costume. In comedy male characters were generally
dressed in a short tunic and cloak, coming down not far below their waist,

with thick tights covering their legs. The costumes were often padded in front and behind to make the actors look short and fat. There were many variations from the basic costume. Actors representing female characters would be dressed accordingly, doubtless with exaggerated features to make it very plain that they were meant to represent females (just as pantomime 'dames' dress for the part today). There would have been special costumes for

20. *Drunken men from Old Comedy: terracotta statuettes*

particular types of character, which all added to the colour and variety. Some idea of the appearance of comic actors is given by fifth-century clay figurines like those in Figure 20 and by the many surviving illustrations of comedies which were performed fifty to a hundred years later in Southern Italy, where some Greeks had settled. The scene from a vase painting in Figure 21 is typical of these. There is no certainty that Aristophanes used costumes exactly like those in South Italian farce but there must have been some similarity.

Comic masks certainly tended to have exaggerated expressions and large mouths. Because characters sometimes represented actual well-known Athenian politicians, their masks took the form of portrait-masks with any prominent features enlarged to create a caricature.

Another essential piece of equipment was the *phallos*. This was a large leather construction which was strapped to the actor's waist, in the form of a man's penis, greatly exaggerated in size. It could be worn tied up, so that it was not too obvious, or it could be loosened for display especially if it was the source of jokes, as it often was. The *phallos* was used to particular effect in Aristophanes' *Women at the Thesmophoria*. In this play a man disguises himself in women's clothes and attends the Thesmophoria, a festival to which only women were admitted. The women are warned that a man is present and, to prove whether this is so, he is stripped by the women. He tries desperately to keep the *phallos* out of sight, as they look first in front and then behind. Eventually, of course, the incriminating evidence is discovered – in a scene which causes great, bawdy merriment.

21. *Comic actors*

This use of the *phallos* has shocked some readers of Aristophanes. Even today, performances of his plays often do not allow actors to wear one and sometimes references to it are omitted from translations. In Victorian times especially the indecency was considered scandalous. Today many people have more relaxed attitudes but it is still hard for us to appreciate that the *phallos* was not included in the plays just in order to obtain an obvious source of cheap laughs. It was strongly associated with the worship of Dionysus, because it was seen as a powerful fertility symbol, standing for life and fruitfulness. At the festivals of Dionysus the god's followers carried huge models of the *phallos* through the city streets, as reminders of the wild, sexual power of the god. It was not considered to be 'obscene' (literally, something not fit for the stage); for the Greeks what was obscene, as we have seen, was the portrayal of violence and death.

The plays

As with tragedy, we can obtain only a partial impression of Greek comedy from reading books about the plays, or reading the plays themselves. So much of comedy depends on visual effects that, for a full appreciation, it is important to watch or even act in live performances. Some videos of modern productions are available, which convey well the often hilarious (as well as occasionally moving and serious) nature of Aristophanes and his plays. Here, it is not possible to deal at length with all the plays, but a short summary of one of them may help us to understand something about the approaches which Aristophanes adopted and the range of his humour.

The Clouds

The Clouds is one of Aristophanes' best-known plays today but it was not a success when it was first produced (423 BC). It came last in the competition and Aristophanes was so disappointed that he rewrote it. The revised version, which we have today, may not have been performed in Aristophanes' lifetime. It is, however, of particular interest because we know a good deal about one of its central characters, the philosopher Socrates, from other Greek writers.

An old Athenian citizen, Strepsiades, has fallen into debt through his son's extravagance. The son, Pheidippides, takes after his mother, who comes from a wealthy family. He is mad about horses – an expensive hobby then as it is now. To help to rescue himself from debt, Strepsiades wants Pheidippides to go to college, to the 'Thinkshop', where Socrates teaches. The reason why Strepsiades believes this will help is that he has heard that Socrates is so clever he can teach students how to make an 'Unfair Argument' defeat a 'Fair Argument'. Pheidippides refuses, so Strepsiades decides to go himself; but he is old and slow and Socrates finds it virtually impossible to teach him anything.

While Socrates tries to get the old man to grasp even the simplest argument, they are watched by the 'Clouds', who give Strepsiades encouragement. The Clouds are the chorus and Aristophanes has chosen them particularly because they can represent a kind of woolly vagueness – just how Aristophanes portrays the wisdom of Socrates. They are supposed to be the new goddesses in whom Socrates and his students believe (they have, it is alleged, got rid of Zeus and the other traditional gods). Eventually, Socrates introduces two characters who represent the Fair and Unfair Arguments. They have a contest which the Unfair Argument wins after a heated debate; this *agon* or central debate was also often found in tragedy, as was seen in *Antigone*. Strepsiades now feels that he is ready to meet the people to whom he owed money and he drives them away with what he imagines are clever examples of the Unfair Argument, though they are actually nonsensical, irrelevant and unintelligent. He demonstrates his new-found 'skills' to Pheidippides. However, the son learns the lessons all too well and is thus able to 'prove' that it is perfectly proper for him to beat Strepsiades, in return for the thrashings which he received from his father when he was a boy. So he starts to beat his father, and this treatment is finally enough to convince Strepsiades that he ought to abandon the Unfair Argument. The play ends as Strepsiades takes his revenge on Socrates by trying to burn down the 'Thinkshop' and angrily chasing away the students of Socrates.

Humour in Aristophanes

The above summary gives some idea of the antics which might go on in a Greek comedy but also suggests that sometimes the humour could be used to make more serious points. It is worth considering some of the forms and targets of Aristophanes' comedy and noting how similar ideas are also found today, although in different contexts.

Satire

In satire, people who are public figures (or their ideas) are ridiculed, often in order to make the audience distrust them or think harder about their ideas. Politicians are a favourite target for satire today, as in Aristophanes' plays. In his days one of the leading politicians was the popular leader Cleon, whom Aristophanes plainly disliked, as well as being opposed to his war policies. Cleon was the subject of some of the playwright's most biting satire (e.g. in *The Knights* and *The Wasps*). *The Clouds* is a satire on the well-known Socrates, but also on a group of philosophers called the Sophists, who taught professionally in Athens. Aristophanes satirises their new ideas, and presents them as dangerously undermining traditional religious beliefs. Satire can be an extremely effective form of opposition. Socrates was certainly damaged by the attacks in *The Clouds*: eventually (399 BC), the Athenians had him sentenced to death for being a bad influence on the young people of the city (like Pheidippides in the play) and for introducing strange religious beliefs in 'new gods' (like the Clouds). He was especially harmed by association with the Sophists. Socrates always maintained that he was very different from the Sophists, since they claimed to be experts and charged high fees for their expertise, whereas he himself never taught professionally or claimed knowledge. However, the effect of the image presented in the play was a very powerful one, whether justified or not. It was mentioned by Socrates in his defence at his trial over twenty years after the play, if we take Plato's *Apology* as an authentic representation of that speech.

Impersonation

Satire often involves impersonation (or an impression) of the person being attacked. The actor who played Socrates doubtless imitated the movements, appearance and voice of the real Socrates; the mask worn by the actor may have reproduced his unusual facial features (Fig. 22). There is a story that

22. *Socrates (469-399 BC)*

Socrates was present at the first performance of *The Clouds* and that he stood up during the play to let himself be seen – perhaps to show the audience what a good likeness it was. Some modern comedians, like Rory Bremner, are well-known for their ability to impersonate and do verbal impressions of famous people such as politicians. Their acts sometimes have a serious point, although some comedians rely mainly on their ability to achieve a convincing likeness. No doubt, politicians are especially pleased with the latter variety of impersonator, since it offers them plenty of additional and not harmful publicity; they thrive on being in the public eye, even though that very publicity may eventually bring them down.

Visual humour

Some things or people are found funny just because they look funny. The old silent films show that visual humour can be of many kinds; they specialise particularly in knockabout, or 'slapstick', comedy – throwing custard pies,

49

slipping on banana skins, or mock violence. In the popular 'Monty Python' comedy shows much of the humour was visual, 'silly walks' for example, or people and objects appearing in unexpected places or situations. There is visual humour in *The Clouds*, as in all Aristophanes' plays: when Socrates makes his first appearance he is swung in front of the *skene* by means of the *mechane*, the crane used for special effects (see Fig. 14, p. 30), sitting in a large basket which is suspended high above the ground.

Verbal humour

Verbal humour such as the use of jokes, puns, silly voices or funny stories relies not on what is seen but on what is said (although, of course, the two types of humour often reinforce each other). Aristophanes was particularly fond of puns (playing on words). It is not difficult to think of comedians today who use puns; sometimes they are deliberately awful, in the expectation that the audience is more likely to groan loudly than to laugh. Puns depend on similarities of words within a language, so they are very difficult to translate exactly from one language to another. As Aristophanes' plays were in Greek, it is hard to appreciate them without knowing that language. At the beginning of *The Clouds* Socrates' students are trying to discover how a gnat sings, in a scene which combines satire with visual humour: does it sing through its mouth or its bottom? The example is intended to show what a waste of time these studies are. They finally decide that the sound emerges from the gnat's backside and there is a pun on the words for 'investigation' and 'bottom', which are similar in Greek. Several translators have tried to reproduce this in English: they call the study an 'intestigation', or refer to 'anal analysis' or an inquiry into 'gnat's agnatomy'. Such attempts are unlikely to provoke any reaction other than a groan.

Topical allusions

Comedy is often about something which is in the current news: this gives rise to many jokes and allusions. In 1998, for example, the World Cup (and in particular the performance of England's team, players and manager) gave rise to many such references; the papers were full of them. Such humour stops being funny very quickly, since it has to be right up to date. Aristophanes' allusions to people or events of nearly 2,500 years ago often do not seem at all amusing now, especially if they need laborious explanation. Modern versions, therefore, tend to leave them out altogether or try to up-date them by substituting contemporary references familiar to the audience – but these, too, can soon become outdated.

Sex and religion

Some subjects are widely regarded as 'taboo'; they are not supposed to be made fun of or discussed in polite company. In many societies, two such subjects are sex and religion, which for the Greeks were very closely connected through the worship of Dionysus as a god of fertility. Today many comedies involve references to sex and religion (perhaps especially sex): 'The Vicar of Dibley' is a recent television comedy where the two subjects sometimes combine. *The Clouds* has some sexual humour, though not as much as some of Aristophanes' other plays. It has considerably more religious references, since new religious ideas were one of the subjects of the play: Aristophanes accuses Socrates of inventing new gods with strange names such as 'Air' and 'Chaos'.

Situation comedy

A common form of comedy which we enjoy today is what is known as 'situation comedy'. The term is a recent invention and the ancient Greeks certainly did not have anything which was the formal equivalent of our modern 'sitcoms', in which the characters are 'ordinary' people to whom slightly extraordinary things seem to happen, when they are trying to deal with the situations and problems of everyday life. Situation comedy can include all of the above types of humour and others, too. We laugh at the characters partly because they are like ourselves, and their problems like our own. We also laugh because they cannot seem to cope with their problems, and in that sense, we may feel 'superior' to them. We think we know what they should do and we laugh because they have not the sense to do it. Although Aristophanes' plays are not 'sitcoms', some of them contain similar elements: that is certainly true of *The Clouds*, which laughs at such familiar situations as that of a husband who marries a wife from a higher social class, with expensive tastes, and a son who squanders his hard-earned money on expensive hobbies. We find it easy to recognise the problems of Strepsiades as those of a mature student who enrols on an educational course and finds it difficult to understand what is going on.

Plays about the war

The war between Athens and Sparta dragged on for twenty-seven years and three of Aristophanes' plays are specifically concerned with attempts to make peace – so much so that it seems the characters' desire for an end to war reflects the poet's own wish and that of many in Athens. In *The Acharnians* (425 BC), an Athenian citizen makes a private peace treaty with the Spartans and other Athenians envy his good fortune. In *Peace* (421 BC), the hero Trygaios fattens up a giant dung beetle to take him to heaven to rescue the goddess Peace, who has been locked away by the god War. The scene where the mechane hoists Trygaios above the *skene*-building on his beetle, who is called Pegasus after the mythical winged horse, is a fine example of visual humour (see Fig. 14, p. 30). The third 'peace play' is *Lysistrata*. This time it is the women who want peace. Lysistrata, an Athenian woman, summons wives not only from Athens but from Sparta and other Greek cities, and persuades them not to have sex with their husbands until the men promise to vote for peace. As the play proceeds, the men grow increasingly frustrated and desperate, while the women still refuse to give in to them (although they do not find this abstinence easy). Finally the men are obliged to agree to the women's demands and the war is ended. *Lysistrata* was written late in the war (411 BC), when things were going badly for the Athenians; hence, in this play, Aristophanes was surely voicing a common desire for peace. What gives the work its originality and humour, of course, is the very idea of a 'general strike' by the women over sex, which has hilarious consequences as its effects on the characters are seen. However, there is an underlying sense of the importance of ending the war which persuades us that the play is more than a bawdy romp, and which ensures that, in our own war-torn world, audiences are no less able to identify with the play's central themes.

Satirical plays

The Clouds makes fun of Socrates but Aristophanes had many other targets, some of which have already been mentioned; one of them was the tragic playwright Euripides. Euripides, many of whose greatest theatrical successes took place at much the same time as those of Aristophanes, features in several of the comedies. Sometimes Aristophanes even includes extracts from his plays in comic situations or imitates his tragic style – a form of comedy known as parody. Many of the audience would have known Euripides' plays very well and seen some of them recently. If they had not been able to recognise them, the point of the parody would have been lost.

Such parody is found particularly in *The Frogs* (405 BC), a play which takes its name from the chorus of frogs whose song ('Brek-ek-ek-ex, ko-ax, ko-ax') accompanies the god Dionysus across the Styx (the river which leads to Hades, the underworld). Dionysus is himself made a figure of fun throughout this play and he had also featured in one of the tragedies of Euripides, *The Bacchants*, written shortly before *The Frogs*. In *The Frogs* Dionysus wishes to bring back from Hades a dead playwright, because he feels that the new writers of tragedy were not good enough to have their plays performed at his festivals. Sophocles and Euripides had both died in 406 BC and Aeschylus had been dead some forty years. In the play there is a competition between Euripides and Aeschylus, to see who is the better playwright and should therefore return to earth. After a long contest (*agon*) Aeschylus wins, as it is felt that his criticisms of the style of Euripides are more effective than the latter's attack on the long words used by Aeschylus.

Euripides features in other plays but the satire is not usually bitter. Aristophanes reserved most of his fiercest criticism for Cleon, particularly because of that politician's determined opposition to peace. There are a number of sneers at the fact that Cleon owned a factory (for tanning the hides of cattle) and therefore came from what might have been considered a rather 'lower class' family, at least by the standards of the upper-class Aristophanes. The attacks are often savage and no doubt they appeared highly amusing to Cleon's political opponents. But Cleon was not amused, and once he was so angry that he summoned Aristophanes before the Council (*Boule*). The attacks continued, however, and the Athenians generally tolerated such abuse in a remarkable way. It is fascinating to compare the freedom of speech enjoyed in Athens by Aristophanes with the limits to which our own comedians may go on television, for example. We have strict laws of libel to protect any politician or other public figure who feels that he/she has been attacked unjustly for immoral behaviour or for swindling the people. In a time of war the limits may be even more sensitive. What would have happened, we may wonder, if a comic playwright had made jokes attacking Churchill's military strategy during the Second World War, or accusing the British themselves of being at least partly to blame for the outbreak of war? Yet this was exactly the kind of attack which Aristophanes made at the height of the war in Athens.

From old to new comedy

In *The Frogs* Dionysus visited the Underworld hoping to bring back a dead playwright. This was impossible even for a god. The great tragic playwrights were gone for ever. The year after *The Frogs* was performed, Athens lost the long war against Sparta. Although Aristophanes carried on writing for a number of years, his work, in an Athens defeated and humiliated in war, started to change in style. His later plays are often referred to as *Middle Comedy*, to distinguish them from the *Old Comedy* which we have been considering. They had lost the political satire and also much of the lively, sometimes farcical quality of the earlier plays. When Aristophanes died in 386 BC (and Fig. 23 may just be his gravestone), the great period of Greek playwriting came to an end. We have only short fragments of the works of the hundreds of comic writers who were active in the fifty years after his death. By the time we reach Menander, the only other Greek comic playwright whose works survive except in fragments, more changes had taken place. We call this last phase of Greek comedy *New Comedy*.

Changes in the theatre

Another important change was in the appearance of the theatres. From the fourth century BC, magnificent stone theatres were built all over Greece and also in Italy and Asia Minor (Turkey). Many of these survive today, in various stages of completeness. One outstanding example, and certainly that best-known by today's tourists, is the superb theatre at Epidauros, in the southern part of Greece (Fig. 24). Today the stage-buildings, which were made of stone, have been almost completely destroyed, but the impressive seating-area and the circular *orchestra* are much as they were when first constructed. As the theatres developed in Roman times, the stage (which had formerly been a low wooden platform) gradually became a four-metre high stone construction, on which all the action took place. The *orchestra* became less important, and

23. *Gravestone of a playwright with comic masks, perhaps Aristophanes, c.380 BC*

hence the original circle was reduced to a semi-circle. This can be seen in the theatre of Dionysus at Athens as it is today and also in the theatre of Delphi (shown in Fig. 25).

The great festivals of Athens were still the centre of dramatic activity, but now professional touring companies took plays all round Greece and to the Greek cities of Southern Italy and Asia Minor. The acting profession began to flourish and soon actors formed themselves into a guild or union, called

The Servants of Dionysus. In many ways, the Greek theatre was still thriving although there were no playwrights to match those of the fifth century BC. The theatre began to rely much more on revivals of the earlier plays, especially those of Aeschylus, Sophocles and Euripides. Euripides, though less popular than the other two in his lifetime, now became the firm favourite – perhaps because his plays seemed more 'modern' in their ideas – with the result that eighteen of his tragedies have survived, more than the total number of surviving plays by Aeschylus and Sophocles together (seven each).

24. *The theatre at Epidauros. View from the east toward auditorium,* orchestra, *and west* parodos *(actors' entrance)*

Menander

The last Greek playwright to be considered here is Menander, who wrote his first play in 321 BC. When he died (about 290 BC) he had written over a hundred of his 'New Comedies', composed for country festivals and perform-ances abroad as well as for the Great Dionysia. In Athens he was not particularly successful: he won the first prize only eight times and in two

25. *Delphi, view of the sanctuary from the top of the theatre*

26. *Menander studying masks for a play. The wide-open mouth and wrinkled fore-head are typical features of the comic masks*

years running came last, in fifth place. Until recently, his plays had almost completely disappeared, but an ancient papyrus-roll was found which contained the text of one whole play, *Dyskolos* (*The Bad-Tempered Man*), and large portions of several others. Menander was greatly admired by the Roman playwrights who are the subject of the next chapter, and they often translated (or more loosely adapted) his plays into Latin. Figure 26 shows Menander in his room, studying possible masks for his characters.

The plays of Menander and other writers of *New Comedy* abandoned the greatly exaggerated costumes of Aristophanes' day. Ordinary clothes were adopted, although masks were still worn. Menander's plays are about ordinary people, too, with themes which affect people of all times and ages: money, romance, bringing up children. The characters were often realistic – they certainly did not act in farcical or ludicrous ways all the time. In some respects, they became more like the characters we recognise from 'soap operas' than the more ridiculous of the 'sitcoms'. The chorus was no longer important and Menander's scripts did not include words for what had by now become only musical interludes. Menander's writing was considered to be of very fine quality, but we have little evidence on which to judge his work properly: only *The Bad-Tempered Man* is complete enough to be acted, and performances are rare. What is clear is that his influence on Roman writers was immense, and it is to these that we shall now turn.

5
Comedy in Rome

Early Italian plays

During the fifth and fourth centuries BC, when Greek drama was at its height, the city of Rome was gradually increasing its power over neighbouring peoples and by the third century BC the Romans controlled all Italy. They took over many ideas from the other people who lived in Italy, especially the Etruscans, who had established an advanced civilisation (with Greek connections) before the Romans conquered them. In addition, the Greeks, who had founded settlements in various parts of the country, especially in the South and in Sicily, had brought over their plays and these were frequently performed as well as becoming the subject of many vase-painting decorations. Even before the full might of the Romans was established, therefore, there was much theatrical activity in Italy.

One popular kind of entertainment was known as the *phlyax*-play – the title coming from a Greek word meaning 'gossip'. *Phlyax*-plays were comical in style, using Greek legends but often changing the stories in humorous ways. Vase-paintings illustrate scenes from these plays as well as tragedies. One of these (Fig. 27) portrays the affair of the chief Roman god Jupiter (Zeus, to the Greeks) with a mortal woman, Alcmena, whom he deceived by disguising himself as her husband, Amphitryo. Alcmena is looking down from a window, while the god Mercury (the Greek Hermes) assists Jupiter by holding out a lamp for him to see where to put his ladder.

Figure 28 provides an interesting example of how we can use such pictures to work out features of the ancient plays, and you might like to consider what can be deduced about what is going on here. (An explanation is given in the Further Study section, see p. 82)

Another kind of dramatic entertainment was the variety of farcical plays which were known as the Atellan plays (from the name of a town in Southern Italy). At first these plays were improvised – there was no script. Later, as their popularity spread, they had written texts. They contained a few popular characters, who appeared regularly; these are what are known as *stock characters* and, to an extent, they are found in all forms of comedy. The stock characters from the Atellan plays were *Pappus* (the grandfather); *Maccus* and *Bucco* (two fools); and *Manducus* (a greedy ogre with great chewing jaws, which could be seen clearly on the masks).

There was also the *mime*, usually presented by a single actor accompanied on the pipes. Mime relies on gesture and facial expression to tell a story and is a distinctive and highly skilled form of acting, as practised, for example, by such modern exponents as Marcel Marceau.

27. *Jupiter and Alcmena*

Roman comedy

While these popular shows all made their contribution to the evolution of Roman comedy, the main ingredient was certainly the Greek *New Comedy* of Menander. All of the plays by the two Roman comic playwrights whose works survive (Plautus and Terence) are translations or adaptations of plays by Menander or his rival playwrights. We cannot tell how much the Roman writers changed the original plays but they could, to some extent, adapt the plots, introduce topical jokes or puns in Latin, and alter the characters.

The theatre in the time of Plautus

Despite the fact that the Greeks had built splendid stone theatres, some of them in Italy, the city of Rome had no permanent theatre at the time of Plautus (who lived from about 240 to 180 BC). Temporary wooden buildings were

28. *Scene from a comedy*

constructed for the performances which were held, in this respect, at least, a little like Greek productions, at festivals in honour of the gods. For his plays Plautus needed a long wooden stage to represent a street and a building behind the stage, which usually showed the fronts of three houses. At each end of the stage there was a side entrance – one used by characters arriving from nearby and one for long-distance travellers. The doors into the houses were used throughout the plays, since all action had to take place in the street. There was little scenery. Because the plays were originally Greek, the scene was usually meant to be Athens or some other part of Greece.

The audience

The playwrights often had a hard time with Roman audiences. At the festivals, various other entertainments also took place. The audience was a mixture of citizens and slaves, women and children, and if a popular attraction turned up at the moment when a playwright was about to present his comedy, there was little that could be done about it. For the Romans, compared with the Greeks, festivals became more like the holidays which we think of when we use the word. People wanted to be amused and playwrights had to take their chance along with jugglers, acrobats, boxers and the rest.

The actors

The position of actors had also changed. In Athens, the winning *protagonist* was something of a hero in the society, but the Romans generally had little respect for actors. Their word for a company of actors was *grex* – which basically refers to a flock of animals such as sheep. Many actors were slaves, or came from the lower classes of citizens. Another change was that the chorus had now disappeared completely from the plays.

The producer

The production was in the hands of the *dominus gregis* ('master of the flock'), who was also usually the chief actor. One of these was Turpio, who produced all of the plays of the second major Roman writer of comedies, Terence (184-160 BC). Turpio would have made a contract with the magistrate who was in charge of the festival; he also hired the actors and arranged rehearsals. It was his duty to provide a musician for the accompaniment: music continued to provide a background for parts of the plays, despite the disappearance of the chorus. Before the production, the playwright sold the play either to the producer or to the festival official; it was then out of his control. He received no more money after a successful performance, or if the play was repeated. If it was a disaster, however, the playwright took no financial risks for it was the producer who stood to lose. So at the start of the play, as leading actor, he would, if necessary, work extremely hard to attract and retain the attention of the fickle audience: sometimes the text includes almost desperate appeals to them to treat the play kindly and not to desert it for other entertainments. The producer had full control over the company. In one play, the producer tells the audience, in an 'aside', that after the performance 'the actors will take their costumes off, and any who have made mistakes with their lines will receive a beating'. He may not have been entirely joking.

Costumes

The basic item of clothing was the tunic – a linen or woollen shirt with holes for the neck and arms. It was pulled on over the head and could be tied with a girdle. Sometimes it was worn by itself, but more often was covered by a

29. *A comic mask*

woollen wrap. The actors wore light sandals and, especially if they represented travellers, sometimes a hat. Actors portraying women were dressed very similarly. These were the clothes of ordinary Greeks and, since the plays came from Greece, the costume was kept. Different types of character might wear special colours: the rich wore purple; prostitutes wore yellow.

The masks also gave the audience an idea of what kind of character to expect. One Roman writer lists forty-four types of mask worn in comedy: eleven for young men, seven for slaves (red-haired, as a rule), three for old women, five for young women, seven for prostitutes, two for slave-girls, and a few others. Figure 29 is a mask for one of the types; you may be able to decide which. Some characters could be recognised from their distinctive 'props'. Soldiers regularly carried swords, cooks had a kitchen knife or spoon. Actors still changed from one part to another, as in the Greek theatre, but this was not so common since there was no longer any rule restricting the cast to three, and actors did not expect very much in the way of payment.

Plautus

Plautus (c. 240-180 BC) was the earlier of the two comic playwrights from Rome whose works survive. Twenty-one of his plays can still be read, the largest number by any ancient playwright, Greek or Roman. These plays typically had rather complicated plots, with various twists and turns, before a happy ending. One of the best-known of Plautus' plays is *Mostellaria*, often known in English as '*The Ghost-Story*'. A summary of its story gives an idea of the kind of plot used by Plautus more generally.

Mostellaria ('*The Ghost-Story*')

Theopropides, an old Athenian gentleman, has been abroad on business for three years. In his absence, his son, a young man called Philolaches, lives a wild life of wine, women and song. A cunning slave, Tranio, has helped Philolaches to free his latest girlfriend, Philematium, from slavery but has had to borrow a large sum from a money-lender in order to do so.

Early in the play a riotous drinking-party takes place, with Philolaches, Philematium and some friends, including one who is very drunk, called Callidamates. Suddenly Tranio arrives with the alarming news that Theopropides is on his way home from the harbour. The revellers panic but Tranio bundles them all inside, telling them to keep completely silent. When the old man arrives Tranio invents a story: the house is haunted by a ghost and is now deserted. There are some slightly embarrassing noises from inside, which make Theopropides rather suspicious, but the wily Tranio is able to convince his old master that these show that the ghost is angry at being disturbed; he tells him that he ought to flee from the ghost's wrath.

Just at this moment the money-lender arrives, demanding payment. Tranio invents more and more lies, saying that Philolaches has had to borrow money to buy a house – the house next door, in fact. Theopropides is about to inspect the house, to see if it is worth buying, when the owner (inevitably) comes home. Tranio's stories become wilder and wilder; the scene and the characters become totally confused. Eventually Theopropides (who has not been particularly quick on the uptake) realises that Tranio has been lying, and threatens to kill him. Tranio flees to the altar for protection. At this point Callidamates, who is now sober, manages to persuade the old man to treat everything as a joke; he settles the financial debts and the play ends happily after all.

Plautus' comedy

Like other comic writers, Plautus relied on many of the forms of humour explored in Chapter 4, except that there was no attempt at satire or serious social comment. The complex plot and its unravelling are central to this style

30. *An old man escorts his drunken son home from a late-night party. The old man (on the right) is looking round anxiously (or angrily?) to see if his son can still walk. The young man has a tambourine in one hand and an oil-lamp in the other. He is wearing a garland on his head, showing that he has been celebrating, and is only just managing to keep his balance*

of comedy. *Mostellaria* is typical of much of the writing of Plautus and *New Comedy* in general. Some of the stock characters are always turning up. There are the old father and the wild son, as shown also in the lively painting of a *phlyax*-play (Fig. 28); and there is the cunning slave, always a very popular character. But Plautus (or perhaps Philemon, who wrote the Greek original) has successfully turned stock characters into amusing individuals, especially

Tranio, one of the best examples of the type. The play relies greatly on visual humour, at which Plautus was particularly skilled. An obvious example is the arrival of the drunken Callidamates. He cannot stand up properly, stammers over his words and does not know where he is.

Most of Plautus' plays have complex plots, involving misunderstandings, mistakes or deception. In *Aulularia* ('*The Pot of Gold*'), there is a miserly old man who thinks that a young man has stolen his gold, when in fact it is his daughter he has stolen. The old man is greatly relieved when he discovers the youth's true motivation. In *The Menaechmi*, twin brothers are reunited after a series of misunderstandings; both have been in the same town, without realising that the other is there, so there are many cases of mistaken identity. Similar confusion is caused in *Amphitryo* (the story illustrated in Fig. 27); when Jupiter disguises himself as Amphitryo to deceive Alcmena, neither the husband nor the wife can work out what has happened; and even more confusion, much like that of the two sets of twins in Shakespeare's *Comedy of Errors*, is caused by Mercury who disguises himself as Amphitryo's slave, Sosia.

Misunderstandings like this are often caused by trickery, such as that of Tranio. In *Miles Gloriosus* ('*The Swaggering Soldier*'), the 'hero' has the splendid name Pyrgopolynices (*pyrgo* means 'tower' or 'battlement' in Greek and *polynices* 'winner of many victories', as well as recalling Polyneices in *Antigone*). Plautus, like many other comic writers, loved long, potentially amusing names. Pyrgopolynices thinks that he is a real lady-killer and is deceived by the wily slave (yet another one), Palaestrio, into thinking that a girl is madly in love with him. However, Palaestrio has also been arranging for the girl to meet her real lover through a hole which has been knocked in the wall between two houses. Pyrgopolynices is made to look a complete fool and the play ends as he thanks his lucky stars that his attempts to seduce the girl have not landed him in any more serious trouble.

Trickery and confusion of this kind had a significant influence on the subsequent development of comedy, and there has already been reference to a similarity with the comedies of Shakespeare, for example. The plays of the French farce writer Feydeau, or the so-called Whitehall farces of Brian Rix, were full of such improbable situations, but they are also found in many other types of comedy. If we think about the plots of sitcoms on television, we will find that they abound in elaborate deceptions, bizarre coincidences and confusion caused by someone's misunderstanding of the situation. In these ways Plautus is certainly a playwright whose comic ideas we can readily recognise.

Terence

Many similar kinds of humour are found in the plays of Terence, who was born at about the time when Plautus died, and this is hardly surprising since they drew on much the same sources. Terence began producing plays when he was only about eighteen but his career was a short one; his last play, *Adelphi* ('*The Brothers*') was written only six years later, not long before he died, still a very young man. *Hecyra* ('*The Mother-in-Law*') was produced three times, because the first two performances were total failures. Terence suffered from the conditions under which Roman comedies were staged. The prologue to the third performance (delivered as usual by his producer, Turpio) explains the nature of the problem:

> Once again I bring you *The Mother-in-Law*. I have never been allowed to present this play in silence; it has been overwhelmed by disasters. If you show your appreciation of our efforts this time, we will undo the damage. The first time I began to act, there was a rumour that some famous boxers, as well as a tight-rope walker, were arriving. Friends started talking to each other, and the women were shouting – so I had to make a premature exit... Well, I tried again later, and everyone enjoyed the opening. But then someone said that there were gladiators on the programme, and people started flooding in to see them, rioting and fighting for seats, with an almighty din. That was the end of *my* little performance.
>
> [Terence, *Hecyra* (the prologue)]

In spite of these difficulties, Terence continued to write. He was more serious than Plautus and perhaps less prepared to give the audience obvious things to laugh at, to keep them on his side. He believed, as Aristophanes had done, that a comic playwright should have something to 'teach' his audience. After his death, his comic ideas had a great influence on later writers and this helped to preserve his six plays for future generations. If he had lived longer there would doubtless have been many more, but he died soon after the first performance of *Adelphi*, supposedly while he was on a journey to Greece – perhaps to seek fresh ideas for plays which he would adapt to the Roman stage. His death definitely marks the end of a chapter, since no later Roman writers' comedies have survived to our times.

6
The end of an era?

Tragedy in Rome

As well as the comedies described in the last chapter, Roman audiences watched tragedies by writers such as Ennius, Pacuvius and Accius. Their plays, from the second century BC, were performed for more than two hundred years, and crowds knew parts of them so well it was said that once, when an actor missed his cue, twelve hundred voices chorused the words. Sadly, apart from a few fragments, these plays, modelled closely on Greek tragedy, have all disappeared but Roman art has many illustrations of tragic actors, such as the striking painting from Pompeii of an actor preparing to put on a mask (Fig. 31).

These tragic masks always had the *onkos*, a raised hairstyle similar to that worn by Roman ladies. An *onkos* – and the high platform shoes (*kothornoi*) which were introduced – made actors look taller, standing out clearly on the high stone stages. It is interesting to compare this picture with the much earlier vase painting of a Greek actor studying his mask (Fig. 10, p. 20). This shows how much the actors' costumes changed over time, and it is important to note that raised hairstyles and high platform boots were never part of the original Greek costume. Figure 32 gives some more examples of Roman masks.

The theatre and the emperors

In 27 BC, Augustus, having defeated Mark Antony in a civil war, became the undisputed ruler of the Roman Empire – its first emperor. The comic and tragic playwrights mentioned above all wrote during the period of the Roman Republic, which ended after Julius Caesar's assassination in 44 BC. Their plays were seen no more, except for occasional revivals; but now, where Plautus and Terence had had to make do with temporary wooden theatre buildings in Rome, gradually the citizens became accustomed to the sight of grand permanent buildings in stone. The first permanent theatre in Rome was the theatre of Pompey, built in 55 BC. During the next hundred years similar buildings spread throughout the Roman Empire. These were in the general style of Greek theatres, but they had fine additional decorations which were pure Roman in conception. In particular, the whole acting area was transformed. Behind the stage, the buildings which formed the background became showpieces of Roman architecture. These features can be seen in Figure 33 – a reconstruction of the so-called theatre of Marcellus in Rome, built during the reign of Augustus. Theatres of this type are found

31. *A tragic actor with his mask*

throughout the Roman empire: that of Herodes Atticus, built beside the old theatre of Dionysus at Athens, is still used for theatrical and operatic performances, as is the well-preserved structure at Orange in southern France.

As these theatres were built the popularity of theatre-going increased, although what audiences went to see had changed considerably. Generally there was less serious drama and more sensational exhibitions, designed to appeal to the less elevated tastes of Roman crowds; few writers now considered writing serious plays. An exception (in the mid-first century AD) was the philosopher and writer Seneca, who was for a while a close adviser of the emperor Nero, until he fell from favour. Seneca was a great student of the

32. *Roman masks*

Greek plays and he composed a number of tragedies which took their inspiration from them. Like many other aristocratic Romans, however, Seneca despised the debased form of entertainment now put on in the theatres. He wrote his plays to be read aloud to select audiences – not for the stage. Like Sophocles, he wrote a play on the story of Oedipus in which he told of the blinding of the king of Thebes: with horrific and lurid descriptions, his work brought out the bloodthirsty and violent elements in the story. His plays were widely read and greatly admired, both in his lifetime and long afterwards. Together with the works of Plautus and Terence, they influenced writers long after the Roman theatres had closed and the Empire had declined and fallen.

The building of stone theatres was accompanied by the growth of huge oval amphitheatres, like the Colosseum in Rome. Like the semicircular theatres, these were also built throughout the Roman empire: that in Figure 34 is in the northern Italian city of Verona. There is even a small one beside the legionary fortress at Caerleon in south Wales (perhaps used as much for soldiers' drill as for theatrical spectacle). In the larger, less provincial amphitheatres, bloody gladiatorial combats and animal-hunts took place. The

33. *The Theatre of Marcellus, Rome*

34. *The Roman amphitheatre, Verona*

crowds loved them, just as they loved the chariot-races which were held in the 'Circuses' (long racecourses, around which teams of horses raced over several laps, as in the famous film *Ben-Hur*). The Roman people had become used to blood and excitement – and the theatre had to cater for such tastes.

Some emperors were themselves devoted to the shows, especially Nero, who thought himself a great singer and actor; but at the time when Nero performed, actors did not take part in the great Greek plays of the past. Instead, there were dramatic recitations of vivid and gory scenes: what the people most liked was to see death and so this is what they were given. Condemned criminals or slaves were actually killed on stage as part of theatrical performances. The same principle applied to sexual displays: live explicit exhibitions on stage were an invention of the Romans. It all seems a long way from the original Greek theatres. People no longer wanted imagination, convention, illusion; they did not want the theatre to imitate life, but to *be* life – and death.

The pantomime

One final highlight of the theatre under the emperors was the *pantomime*, which developed partly from the original *mime*. The central figure in the pantomime was a masked dancer, who performed scenes with no words, accompanied by a musician with pipes. Poor poets could make a great deal of money from writing lyrics for the chorus who sang in the background. The pantomime actor himself (it was always a man) was a handsome, athletic figure who wore a graceful silk costume; his movements were artistic and flowing. Although he acted out scenes from Greek mythology, his appeal was very different from that of the tragic actors. Like a modern pop-singer, he attracted vast numbers of fans (of both sexes) who practically worshipped him. One pantomime star named Paris even had an affair with the emperor's wife, which led to her banishment from Rome; he himself was executed. On his tombstone was an inscription which he had composed for himself. He called himself 'the glory of the theatre'.

The end of the Roman theatre

The theatre under the emperors had changed almost beyond recognition but it was far from dead: the splendid theatre buildings were frequently full. Slaves known as 'comic actors' entertained guests at the banquets of the rich. However, once Christianity spread and gained power in the Empire (becoming the official Roman religion under the emperor Constantine in the fourth century AD), theatre-going was heavily criticised as immoral. Finally, in the sixth century AD, a Christian emperor, Justinian, closed down the theatres – despite the fact that he was married to a former mime actress, Theodora, whose strip-tease act had been very popular.

The plays go underground

After the fall of the Roman Empire there came the period known as the 'Dark Ages'; invasions by barbarians from the north and east practically put a stop to the study of literature and the other arts. Some Greek and Roman manuscripts survived and many monks spent their lives copying them out, often without understanding what they were writing. Acting itself did not die out entirely during this period. Even though the theatre buildings were closed, actors and mime artists could still perform in country districts and simple settings, keeping alive the traditions and characters of the old theatre.

The Renaissance

The Renaissance (literally, 'rebirth') was the period when an interest in creating works of art and literature reawakened in Europe, largely through the fact that some people had continued to study Greek and Roman writers. The Renaissance started in the fourteenth century and, by the fifteenth, Italian writers were producing Latin plays, which were influenced by the Roman playwrights. In Italy, performances recommenced of the Roman comedies: the Pope watched Plautus' *The Menaechmi* at the Vatican in 1502. The movement spread to Germany, Holland and England, helped greatly by the invention of the printing press. Oxford and Cambridge universities and famous English schools started to perform Roman plays. In 1527 St Paul's School in London produced *The Menaechmi*, and in the following year Terence's *Andria*. Seneca's influence was also felt and his at times horrific, gruesome tragedies were copied in Italian plays of the sixteenth century.

Shakespeare

In the same period, Seneca's plays were also being read and even performed in England. Shakespeare himself was strongly influenced by them; in *Hamlet*, Polonius says: 'Seneca cannot be too heavy nor Plautus too light.' Playwrights thought that the Roman writers were ideal models to follow and Shakespeare's tragedies (*King Lear*, for example) contain bloody scenes, stories of revenge and violence. Despite the fact that he was said to know 'small Latin and less Greek', Shakespeare certainly read plays by Plautus and Terence at school; they were part of the basic curriculum. *The Comedy of Errors* is based largely on Plautus' *The Menaechmi* and *Amphitryo*, and in many other plays ideas were taken from New Comedy. There are all the familiar motifs: exchanges of character, mistaken identity, long-lost children being reunited, and many other of the basic ingredients we have met. Some characters even have names from the Roman plays: in *The Taming of the*

Shrew there are servants called Tranio and Grumio. Shakespeare also uses the stock characters such as the boasting soldier, the most famous being Falstaff in *Henry IV*.

Other influences

The Romans also influenced other English writers of Shakespeare's day, such as Marlowe and Ben Jonson, and eighteenth-century writers like Sheridan, author of *The Rivals* and other comedies. In France in the seventeenth century, Molière's comedies owed much to Roman comedy, while Corneille and Racine modelled their tragedies on those of the Greeks. In Italy, the *Commedia dell' Arte*, which included a number of famous stock characters like Harlequin and Columbine, had ideas which seem to go right back to the very earliest examples of the Italian theatre, the Atellan plays. In the late eighteenth century, the German poet and playwright Goethe wrote an influential version of the play by Euripides, *Iphigenia among the Taurians*.

Even architecture showed the influence of the ancient theatre. The Globe Theatre in London, used by Shakespeare and now restored to its original form, was in a quite different style and shape. However, Shakespeare, like Sophocles, wrote for an open-air theatre with little scenery to assist him. Both relied, as we have seen, on the actors' words and the audience's imagination, not on tremendous scenic effects such as those sometimes seen in modern productions. In part the Renaissance was also an architectural 'rebirth', and the Italian architect Palladio studied closely ancient styles and designs. He based the Teatro Olimpico at Vicenza in Italy on the plans of the Roman architect Vitruvius, and a famous production of Sophocles' *Oedipus the King* was performed there in 1585, to inaugurate the building. This, however, was a very unusual event, as such live performances of the Greek tragedies themselves did not take place on a significant scale for more than two hundred years after that.

The twentieth century

When we come down to the twentieth century, we find that not only has the influence of the Greek and Roman theatre survived, in many ways it has been revived to an extent never previously seen. This is true both of plays written today and in the performance of classical works, either in the original or in translation. Many modern plays still use the themes and ideas of the Greeks and Romans. A recent French writer, Jean Giraudoux, called one of his plays *Amphitryon 38*, because it was the thirty-eighth known play on the legend (the first being Plautus' *Amphitryo*). Anouilh's *Antigone* was based closely on the version by Sophocles but with important changes of emphasis, and Oedipus was also an inspiration for two important French plays: André

Gide's *Oedipe* and Jean Cocteau's *La Machine Infernale*. A particularly popular choice of subject-matter has been the story of Electra and Orestes, daughter and son of King Agamemnon and Queen Clytemnestra of Mycenae – a subject used by Aeschylus, Sophocles and Euripides. The American playwright Eugene O'Neill wrote *Mourning Becomes Electra* after reading the plays of Aeschylus, but set his own version in New England, USA, at the end of the American Civil War; this was an attempt not simply to re-use the story but to give it a completely modern context. Other writers such as T.S. Eliot (*The Family Reunion*) and the French philosopher and writer Jean-Paul Sartre (*Les Mouches*) were also strongly influenced by Aeschylus. After more than two millennia of virtual neglect by writers, the satyr-play gave rise to Tony Harrison's extraordinary *The Trackers of Oxyrhynchus*, which received its first performance at Delphi in Greece in 1988.

Performances of Greek and Roman plays

With so many good translations available, the plays are often performed today. The staging in the 1980s by Sir Peter Hall of the full trilogy by Aeschylus (the *Oresteia*), using masks, was a landmark in showing how powerful the experience of watching Greek drama could be. This gave rise to other attempts to recreate the idea of a sustained viewing experience, especially the Royal Shakespeare Company's production, *The Thebans*, which put together the three plays of Sophocles, *Oedipus the King*, *Oedipus at Colonus* and *Antigone.* The performance lasted six-and-a-half hours. Several excellent films have been made of the Greek tragedies: the Italian director Pasolini produced a gripping version of Sophocles' *Oedipus the King.* Television and radio have also brought the classical works to today's audiences. There are even productions which use the original language of the plays, particularly in schools (see Figs. 15, p. 33 and 17, p. 38) and in universities.

Other links

These productions help to keep alive the spirit of the ancient theatre but there are many other modern links, perhaps less obvious. It is with opera that the link to Greek and Roman theatre is particularly strong, and in certain respects that combination of words, music and movement is closer to the full Greek theatrical production than are our modern plays. Many operas, from those of Monteverdi in the sixteenth century to Stravinsky in the twentieth, have taken their subjects directly from the Greeks and Romans. Nor is the link only with tragedy. Millions of people in Britain and America each year watch the comic operettas of Gilbert and Sullivan, but how many of them see the connection between them and the plays of Aristophanes and Plautus? The boasting soldiers who are stock characters in New Comedy, and also in Shakespeare, turn up yet again in several of these operas. *HMS Pinafore* and *The Gondo-liers* both have plots based on mixing up babies at birth. When Gilbert makes fun of British law courts (*Trial by Jury*), politics and politicians (*Iolanthe*), or dreamy intellectuals (*Patience*), he is close to the spirit of *The Acharnians*, *The Wasps* and *The Clouds*.

To come right up to date, we have only to think of the many comedy programmes on television that owe their ideas to humour which, if not as old as the hills, is certainly as old as the ancient Greeks. This book has referred to some recent examples but they can quickly become outdated, replaced by new variations – often on exactly the same themes and characters.

Conclusions

This chapter is called 'The End of an Era?' and, in some ways, the theatre of the Greeks and Romans has certainly gone for ever. Perhaps we shall never fully understand what a Greek who attended the Great Dionysia festival felt, in the Athens of the fifth-century BC – not least because, for us, going to the theatre is no longer a religious activity. Worldwide, few people take part in religious ceremonies which are like those of the Greeks. It is impossible to imagine completely the thoughts or feelings of an actor such as Dicaiarchos, who may have played a dozen parts, old and young, male and female, in a single day. And we have also lost sight of the idea of theatre-going as some-thing which involves a very large proportion of society. Today only a small minority of the population ever sets foot in a theatre to see a play.

Not everything is remote or difficult to grasp, however; audiences still laugh at comedies and are moved by tragedies, in the theatre or cinema, on radio or television. In many ways there is more opportunity than ever before for those who wish to take part in plays – whether in schools or dramatic societies. Even if actors rarely wear actual masks, the experience of an actor in seeking to impersonate a character is essentially much the same.

A long road leads from Athens and the theatre of Dionysus to our modern theatres and television plays – but it will certainly go much further, thanks to the endless fascination of drama and the stage.

Bibliography

For teachers

Volume I of the splendid *Cambridge History of Classical Literature: Greek Literature*, edited by P.E. Easterling and B.M.W. Knox (Cambridge University Press, 1985), is admirably authoritative. For festivals, performances and costume, see especially A.W. Pickard-Cambridge's enormously thorough work, *The Dramatic Festivals at Athens*, revised by J. Gould and D.M. Lewis (Oxford University Press, 1968). R. C. Flickinger's *The Greek Theater and its Drama* (Chicago University Press, 1918) is still very useful, and so is *An Introduction to the Greek Theatre* by P.D. Arnott (Macmillan, 1959) – which could well be read by older pupils. A most valuable book on Greek Tragedy for teachers is the excellent collection of essays in *The Cambridge Introduction to Greek Tragedy* (ed. P.E. Easterling, Cambridge University Press, 1997), and another is S. Goldhill, *Reading Greek Tragedy* (Cambridge University Press, 1986). The Dionysiac aspects of the Greek theatre are explored provocatively in R. Seaford's *Reciprocity and Ritual. Homer and Tragedy in the Developing City-State* (Oxford University Press, 1994); *Tragedy in Athens* by D. Wiles (Cambridge University Press, 1997) is a stimulating, up-to-date treatment, as is E. Csapo and W.J. Slater, *The Context of Ancient Drama* (Ann Arbor, 1995).

Among general books on tragedy and comedy, there are two good short works in the, alas, discontinued *Ancient Culture and Society* series (Chatto & Windus): *The Greek Tragic Theatre,* H.C. Baldry (1971), and *The Comic Theatre of Greece and Rome*, F.H. Sandbach (1977). These are designed especially for students undertaking more advanced studies at school or university. H.D. Kitto's *Form and Meaning in Drama* (Methuen, 1956) is a deservedly popular treatment of several plays, including *Antigone*; R. Lattimore's *Story Patterns in Greek Tragedy* (Athlone Press, 1964) has an interesting discussion of the plots. On Greek comedy, P.A. Cartledge, *Aristophanes and his Theatre of the Absurd*, in the *Classical World* series (BCP, 1990), is informed by recent scholarship. Others include *Aristophanes* by G. Murray (Oxford University Press, 1933), *The Stage of Aristophanes* by C.W. Dearden (Athlone Press, 1976), and K.J. Dover's *Aristophanic Comedy* (Batsford, 1972) and are all very well worth reading. On Roman comedy, W. Beare's *The Roman Stage* (Methuen, 1969) is comprehensive, while also very interesting are *Roman Laughter* by E. Segal (Harvard University Press, 1968), and G.E. Duckworth's *The Nature of Roman Comedy* (Princeton University Press, 1962).

Many of these books are well illustrated, but some of the best collections of the visual evidence are still to be found in *The History of the Greek and Roman Theater* by M. Bieber (Princeton University Press, 1961); and *Illustrations of Greek Drama* by A.D. Trendall and T.B.L. Webster (Phaidon, 1971). J.R. Green's *Theatre in Ancient Greek Society* (London University Press, 1994) is a valuable addition; the same author collaborated with E. Handley in *Images of the Greek Theatre* (London, British Museum Press, 1995). The visual evidence receives an excellent discussion in the chapter 'The Pictorial Record' in *The Cambridge Companion to Greek Tragedy*, by O.P. Taplin. The same author has written excellent books on performance aspects of the Greek theatre: *Greek Tragedy in Action* (London University Press, 1978) and *The Stagecraft of Aeschylus* (Oxford University Press, 1977).

Of the numerous editions of the plays, two are perhaps worthy of particular mention for use with older students: *The Clouds*, edited by K.J. Dover (Oxford University Press 1968) and Sophocles' *Electra* by J.H. Kells (Cambridge University Press, 1973). A useful edition of *Antigone* is by A.L. Brown (Warminster, 1988).

Translations abound. Those in the Loeb Classical Library (with parallel text and translation) cover the whole range but are not the most readable. The series *The Complete Greek Tragedies* (edited by D. Grene and R. Lattimore) (Chicago University Press, 1953-59) is generally good, and there is a useful translation of all of Aristophanes' comedies by P. Dickinson, in two volumes (Oxford University Press, 1970). More suitable for acting perhaps are the Penguin versions, which cover the full range and are generally produced with performance in mind. Penguin also include Aristotle's *Poetics*, the *locus classicus* for theories of tragedy, in *Classical Literary Criticism* (T.S. Dorsch, 1965). Two useful sets of translations by K. McLeish are Sophocles: *Electra, Antigone, Philoctetes*; and Aristophanes, *Clouds, Women in Power, Knights* (Cambridge University Press, 1978). A helpful introductory anthology, with some plays translated into English and extracts from others, is *Greek Drama for Everyman* by F.L. Lucas (Dent, 1954). T. Harrison's enterprising version (London University Press, 1981) was used for the celebrated production of *The Oresteia* by Sir Peter Hall.

Finally, there are two excellent surveys of the literature available, at the time of compilation, in the series *New Surveys in the Classics* (Oxford University Press): *Greek Tragedy* by T.B.L. Webster (1971), and *Menander, Plautus, Terence* by W.G. Arnott (1975).

For students

A simple introduction, especially for younger students, is given in *The Greek Theatre* (*Aspects of Greek Life* series, Longman, 1972) by K. McLeish. The same author has also written the fuller, more detailed *Roman Comedy* (*Inside the Ancient World* series, Macmillan, 1976). His simplified translations of several plays are in two volumes in *The Heritage of Literature*, a series by Longman. In *Four Greek Plays*, there is a version of *Antigone* which is certainly the most accessible for acting by younger pupils; the other collection is *The Frogs and Other Plays*. For older pupils, the series *Classical World* (BCP/Duckworth, edited by Michael Gunningham), is indispensable for classical studies, with the useful *Greek Tragedy: an Introduction*, by M. Baldock and Paul Cartledge's *Aristophanes and His Theatre of the Absurd* immediately relevant.

Many books about the history of the theatre have a chapter on the Greek and Roman theatre, such as *Discovering the Theatre* by C.V. Burgess (University of London Press, 1960). There are excellent illustrations of the theatre throughout history in *Theatres: An Illustrated History* by S. Tidworth (Pall Mall Press, 1973) and *World Theatre, an Illustrated History* by B. Gascoigne (Ebury Press, 1968).

Among the historical novels which deal with related topics are *The Mask of Apollo* by M. Renault (Longman, 1968), already quoted in this book. *The Crown of Violet* by G. Trease (Macmillan, 1961) has an imaginative, though not always accurate, account of a festival.

Further Study

Topics for discussion

1. What kind of people in our society become 'stars', and how? What kind of followers do they attract, and what is their attraction? Select a list of, for example, 'ten famous stars', and compare this with those produced by others in your class. Are they similar or different? Does either list contain any actors or actresses? Why do you think this is?

2. What are the advantages and disadvantages of an outdoor theatre? What would your ideal theatre be like?

3. Discuss the topics raised by reading or seeing the play *Antigone*.

4. Do you think there is too much sex in comedies or television plays today? Why is sex such a popular subject for humour? What about religion? Should humour be 'politically correct'? Should any kinds of humour be banned because they are offensive to some people?

5. How much freedom of speech is there in your country today, in the theatre and on television or radio? How does this compare with the theatre of Aristophanes? Should there be any restrictions on what is said or shown on stage? Why?

Subjects to write about or research

1. Choose one character from a modern comedy (for example, on radio or television). Describe this person in detail, mentioning appearance, personality and any other features which you think are important. To what extent does the personality of the person playing the part come through? Do you think the actor or actress resembles the character portrayed? Why? What skills does an actor need to create a different character?

2. Compare (with illustrations) the costume of a clown with that of a Greek comic actor. How different are they? Which is funnier to look at, and which is the more complete disguise?

3. Using the Greek alphabet (Appendix II), decipher what you can of the fragment of the *Athenian Victors' List* (page 5). Using Greek letters, write the numbers 24, 13 and 7. Write in Greek the names of Antigone, Creon and Haimon. How did the English words *orchestra, scene, theatre* and *hypocrite* come to have their present meanings? How much have these changed since the time of the ancient Greeks? Why have these changes taken place?

79

4. Research into other words which have their origins in Greek, and see if any similar changes have taken place.

5. Imagine that you have been appointed *choregos* for *Antigone*. Write a plan of your activities in the period leading up to the performance, describing how you intend to help Sophocles to win.

6. Analyse the success of some modern comedians, explaining clearly what makes them successful and what kinds of humour they use.

7. Find out what you can about festivals in different countries today, looking at their religious significance and how they are celebrated. Discover any links with theatrical performances.

8. Research into films and plays about the legendary heroes of your own country, and consider how the heroic characters are portrayed.

9. Discover what you can about the design of theatre buildings today, and about how theatres are organised. How are theatres financed? How much does it cost to go to the theatre? Where do the actors come from? What kinds of plays are produced, who goes to the theatre, and what are the most popular forms of production? How long do plays 'run' when they appear in the theatre?

Practical activities

1. Make a model of a Greek theatre, such as the theatre of Dionysus. (You may use the plan and photographs in this book.)

2. Sophocles invented the practice of painting the front wall of the *skene*-building. From what you have learnt about the play, produce an illustration to show the kind of painting which you think would have been suitable for a production of *Antigone.*

3. Working in a group of three, study *Antigone*, and decide on how to divide the parts among the three.

4. Imagine that you are Dicaiarchos, playing the four parts in *Antigone* which are listed on page 29. Work out how to play the four different characters, thinking about their voices, walks, personalities and gestures. See if your friends can tell which you are supposed to be from your movements, or from your voice. Reverse roles with others in the group.

5. Using illustrations from vase-paintings, or books about the theatre, design and (if possible) make costumes for *Antigone*.

6. Again working from illustrations you have seen, design and make a tragic or comic mask to suit one of the characters you have read about. (A group could perhaps make masks for all of the characters in *Antigone*.)

7. Act out a scene from a tragedy, wearing a mask. Decide how you will present various emotions without being able to use facial expressions, eg: laughter, crying, astonishment, horror, bewilderment. Discuss the experience of acting in a mask: did this help you to feel a sense of being someone other than yourself? Why?

8. Study the messenger-speech from *Antigone* telling of the death of Antigone and Haimon. Plan how to make this dramatically effective (movement, tone of voice, use of pauses, changes of speed, for example), and present it to your group.

9. Using the illustrations you have seen as an example, design and paint a scene from *The Clouds* to go on the side of a Greek vase.

10. Construct a miniature working model of a *mechane* that is capable of hoisting a small figure into the air and moving it across a stage. Think about the technology involved: how might this enable us to make a *mechane* better or differently from the Greeks?

11. Read a myth or legend written by the ancient Greeks, and write a play (tragedy or comedy) based on it. Follow the Greek rules for the number of actors, and introduce some choral scenes for singing and dancing.

12. Act out a scene (or, if possible, more – or even the whole play) from one of the comedies of Aristophanes. Work out how to make it funny to the audience (without, of course, making it silly). Try to update some of the humour to include topical references.

13. In a group, prepare to present a chorus from a Greek tragedy. If possible, use fifteen chorus-members, with others to assist with the production by preparing music, making costumes and masks, working out the choreography and training the chorus. Use an oboe, flute or recorder to accompany the music, perhaps with a small drum to help with the rhythm. Some of the class may be able to compose suitable music. Think out the dances and movements, and practise good chorus and solo effects, and variations in mood and volume. One simple idea to get started is to take the very 'hymn-like' translation of a chorus from Antigone on pages 34–5. The tune below may give you an idea. Notice that on a piano only white notes are needed. However, if each note is treated as a 'sharp', the tune can be played entirely on the five black notes (the 'pentatonic scale').

The picture on page 60

This is supposed to show an old miser who is being robbed by two thieves. The figure on the right, looking on, appears to be a slave, and a rather useless one. The old man sleeps on a large box containing his treasures, to protect them. The thieves are trying to pull him off, but are tugging in opposite directions.

Appendix I

Plays and playwrights

This Appendix contains the titles of Greek and Roman plays which have survived to the present day and the names of their authors. In brackets are the approximate dates of the authors and of the first performances of the plays (when these are reasonably certain). If a play is named after a central character, this Greek or Roman name is given as the title; otherwise, an English translation is given.

Greek tragedy

Aeschylus (525-456 BC). First victory in a dramatic competition: 484 BC
The Persians (472); *Seven against Thebes* (467); *The Suppliants* (463); *Agamemnon, The Libation-Bearers, The Kindly Ones* (*The Oresteia,* or Oresteian trilogy) (458); *Prometheus Bound.*

Sophocles (496-406 BC). First victory, 468 BC
Ajax; Antigone (442?); *Oedipus the King* (430-428?); *Women of Trachis; Electra* (413?); *Philoctetes* (409); *Oedipus at Colonus.*

Euripides (485-406 BC). First victory, 441? BC
Rhesus; Alcestis (438); *Medea* (431); *Children of Heracles* (430-428?); *Hippolytus* (428); *Andromache* (425?); *Hekabe* (before 423?); *Suppliant Women* (423?); *Electra* (before 415?); *The Mad Heracles* (before 415?); *Trojan Women* (415); *Iphigenia among the Taurians* (413); *Helen* (412), with *Andromeda* and *Cyclops* (satyr-play)?; *Ion; Phoenician Women; Orestes* (408); *Iphigenia at Aulis* and *The Bacchants* (both produced after Euripides' death).

Greek comedy

Aristophanes (450-386 BC). First victory, 425 BC
The Acharnians (425); *The Knights* (424); *The Clouds* (423); *The Wasps* (422); *Peace* (421); *The Birds* (414); *Lysistrata* (411); *Women at the Thesmophoria* (411); *The Frogs* (405); *Women in the Assembly* (392); *Wealth* (388).

Menander (342-290 BC). First victory, 317 BC
The Bad-Tempered Man (317); parts of *The Arbitrants* and *Women from Samos.*

Roman comedy

Plautus (240-180 BC)

The Donkeys; The Pot of Gold; Amphitryo; The Bacchis Sisters; The Prisoners; Casina; The Little Box; Curculio; Epidicus; The Menaechmi; The Merchant; The Swaggering Soldier; The Ghost-Story; The Persian; The Little Carthaginian; Pseudolus; The Rope; Stichus; Three Pieces of Silver; Truculentus; The Travelling Bag.

Terence (184-160 BC)

Women from Andros (166); *The Mother-in-Law* (165); *The Self-Torturer* (163); *The Eunuch* (161); *Phormio* (161); *The Brothers* (160).

Roman tragedy

Seneca (4 BC – AD 65)

Hercules; Trojan Women; Phoenician Women; Medea; Phaedra; Oedipus; Agamemnon; Thyestes.

Appendix II

The Greek alphabet

This alphabet is fairly easy to learn, even for those who are not intending to study ancient Greek; several examples have been used in this book. It is also used by mathematicians, and of course in modern Greece. Notice that Greek has seven vowels, with a short *e* and a long *e*, and a short *o* and a long *o*.

Capital letter	Small letter	English equivalent
A	α alpha	a (h*a*t)
B	β beta	b
Γ	γ gamma	g (*g*et)
Δ	δ delta	d
E	ε epsilon	e (b*e*t)
Z	ζ zeta	z
H	η eta	(b*ee*)
Θ	θ theta	th
I	ι iota	i (h*i*t)
K	κ kappa	k, c (*c*at)
Λ	λ lambda	l
M	μ mu	m
N	ν nu	n
Ξ	ξ xi	x
O	o omicron	o (h*o*t)
Π	π pi	p
P	ρ rho	r
Σ	σ (ς) sigma	s
T	τ tau	t
Y	υ upsilon	u, y
Φ	φ phi	ph
X	χ chi	ch (lo*ch*)
Ψ	ψ psi	ps (li*ps*)
Ω	ω omega	(g*o*)

Index